STEPPING FORWARD TOGETHER

Joshua Stepping Forward into the Jordan

Joshua leads priests into the Jordan River. He splits the waters.
Jericho is represented over his shoulder.

STEPPING FORWARD TOGETHER

SYNAGOGUE VISIONING AND PLANNING

Second Edition

ROBERT LEVENTHAL

With Aimee Close and the
United Synagogue of Conservative Judaism
Department of Synagogue Leadership

Foreword by Rabbi Jacob Blumenthal

ROWMAN & LITTLEFIELD
Lanham • Boulder • New York • London

Published by Rowman & Littlefield
An imprint of The Rowman & Littlefield Publishing Group, Inc.
4501 Forbes Boulevard, Suite 200, Lanham, Maryland 20706
www.rowman.com

6 Tinworth Street, London SE11 5AL, United Kingdom

An earlier version of chapter 15 was published by Aimee Close in
eJewishPhilanthropy in December 2018.

An earlier version of chapter 19 was published by Aimee Close in
eJewishPhilanthropy in 2019.

British Library Cataloguing in Publication Information Available

Library of Congress Cataloging-in-Publication Data

Names: Leventhal, Robert F., author. | Close, Aimee, author. | Blumenthal,
Jacob, writer of added foreword. | United Synagogue of Conservative
Judaism. Department of Synagogue Leadership, author.
Title: Stepping forward together : synagogue visioning and planning / Robert
Leventhal ; with Aimee Close and the United Synagogue of Conservative
Judaism Department of Synagogue Leadership; foreword by Rabbi Jacob
Blumenthal.
Other titles: Stepping forward
Description: Second edition. | Lanham : Rowman & Littlefield, [2020] | Includes
bibliographical references and index.
Identifiers: LCCN 2020012909 (print) | LCCN 2020012910 (ebook) | ISBN
9781538142592 (cloth) | ISBN 9781538142608 (paperback) | ISBN
9781538142615 (epub)
Subjects: LCSH: Synagogues—Organization and administration. | Jewish
leadership.
Classification: LCC BM653 .L36 2020 (print) | LCC BM653 (ebook) | DDC
296.6/5—dc23
LC record available at https://lccn.loc.gov/2020012909
LC ebook record available at https://lccn.loc.gov/2020012910

*This book is dedicated to those leaders
who have been willing to work through
the initial resistance and the short-term chaos of planning
to create something new, to step forward.*

Sources

Scripture quotations, unless otherwise noted, are reprinted from the Tanakh, © 1999, The Jewish Publication Society, with the permission of the publisher, The Jewish Publication Society.

Other ancient sources are generally from Shlomo Toperoff, *Avot: A Comprehensive Commentary on the Ethics of Our Fathers* (Northvale, NJ: Jason Aronson, 1997); *The Soncino Talmud* (Chicago: Judaica Press, 1995); and Hayim Nahman Bialik and Yehoshua Hana Ravnitzky, eds., *The Book of Legends: Legends from the Talmud and Midrash*, translated by William G. Braude (New York: Schocken Books, 1992).

Transliterations are based on the romanization table of Yale University Press.

The frontispiece is reproduced with permission of the artist, Barbara Leventhal Stern, Palo Alto, California, artbabe51@aol.com.

Contents

PART I

Thriving Synagogues and Their Leaders

PART II

Understanding the Lay of the Land

PART III

Getting Organized for the Journey

PART IV
Making Meaning of Information

PART V
Lessons Learned

Background and Acknowledgments

Background

Gratitude

Having a grateful heart gives you energy. In the mystical tradition angels on earth are here to encourage our goodness. Some believe that angel specialists encourage our faith, our study, and our service. As I stepped forward from the world of business into the uncertain waters of consulting, I needed a host of angel specialists. We are taught that when we see someone stranded on the roadside, we are to stop our journey and help them with theirs. These angels got off of their carts to help raise me up.

I started on the side of the road as a very peripheral Jew. In my thirties I became involved in my Jewish community center and in a Jewish Federation campaign. In my early forties I went on the national United Jewish Appeal Young Leadership Cabinet and was involved in Israel advocacy. In my mid-forties I turned to the realm of Jewish education. I became the president of the board of my local day school. In my late forties I volunteered to be the seventh-grade teacher in our supplementary two-day religious school. What makes someone move from the periphery of Jewish practice and community to the center? I will return to this question throughout the book. My interest is more than academic. I am trying to look at my own roadmap and understand how a Jewish businessman from Dayton, Ohio, journeyed to the nation's largest Protestant consulting firm and created a practice of synagogue consulting. I am convinced that my journey was shaped by various angels.

I was first encouraged in Jewish communal life by our Federation's executive director, Peter Wells. I was recruited to develop a synagogue leadership program by my rabbi, Irving Bloom. I was supported in my Judaic training by my graduate school advisor at Spertus Institute, Dr.

Elliot Lefkovitz. As a seventh-grade teacher, I was mentored by Temple Israel's educator, Rabbi Jennifer Marx Asch. I also want to thank the entire faculty of the Union for Reform Judaism's Sh'liach Kehillah program for two extraordinary summer workshops.

My synagogue consulting practice could not have developed without the generous support of STAR (Synagogue Transformation and Renewal). I would like to thank the Charles H. Schusterman Foundation, the Bronfman Foundation, and the Jewish Life Network (Michael Steinhardt) for their early support of the Alban consulting project.

As I developed my consulting, I was supported by the Rev. John Janka and Dr. Gil Rendle of the Alban Institute. My guide to the world of synagogue conflict was the Rev. Speed Leas. I was inspired by the workshop I took on Future Search with Marvin Weisbord and Sandra Janoff. This gave me a vision of the energy of large-group stakeholder workshops. I have adapted their tools and blended them with others. I received input from such thoughtful readers as Jerry Garfield, Alice Mann, Susan Beaumont, Kathryn Palen, and Larry Peers.

I am grateful to the following people for enabling me to adapt my planning work to USCJ from 2013 to 2019: Rabbi Steven Wernick hired me and gave me a free hand to develop the leadership toolbox I had started at the Alban Institute. I was supported in that work by Kathy Elias and Rabbi Charles Savenor. In 2012 I was asked to develop a USCJ version of synagogue visioning and planning that we called Sulam for Strategic Planners.

In 2014 I was joined by three USCJ colleagues, Aimee Close, Jay Weiner, and Nadine Kochavi. Together we have worked with more than sixty congregations over the past six years. We have built on the planning tools that I outlined in my original book. We committed to continuous improvement. We tweaked some exercises, made major changes to others, and added some entirely new elements. I am indebted to their courageous workshop leadership and to their efforts in building and refining this planning process.

I would like to thank USCJ Chief Operating Officer, Leslie Lichter, for supporting this book development project and Rabbi Joshua Rabin for being a careful reader.

Finally, I would like to thank my wife, Carolyn, and my three boys, Daniel, Micah, and Eli, for their support, and my mother, Shirley Leventhal, and my father, Harry Leventhal, both of blessed memory, for my love of Judaism.

Foreword
Rabbi Jacob Blumenthal

Before taking on my current role in the Rabbinical Assembly, I spent over twenty joyful years as a congregational rabbi in the Maryland suburbs of Washington, DC. When I led the first High Holidays of my congregation as a student rabbi, I could not have imagined what that core group might become. It was a wonderful group of twenty or so families, meeting in a school cafeteria in a new suburb. A few dozen of us sang together, studied together, celebrated our small children, and wondered if we had a future. Over time we welcomed hundreds of individuals and families, established vibrant educational and prayer experiences, built a permanent home, did countless kind things for each other and the larger community, and formed an enduring network of relationships.

During these years I experienced what it was like to be at the founding of a community. I watched as we grew, learning by trial and error. In time, I developed the capacity to manage a more mature congregation. At each stage I was challenged to reflect on our situation and look for our next chapter. This book encourages this kind of reflection. What I learned over those two decades, including many strategic planning conversations and processes, is that there is a difference between "sight" and "vision." One may see something clearly, but vision requires imagination—a sense of what is possible.

One of my favorite *piyyutim* (prayer poems) on Yom Kippur is "*ki hinei kahomer*," in which we imagine ourselves as raw material that God shapes over the course of a given year. We imagine ourselves as clay, and God as the potter; ourselves as glass, and God as the glazier. It is a poem that sees God as visionary Creator, helping us recreate our lives. It is a poem that celebrates vision and pushes us to see beyond the current flawed people we are in that moment and imagine who we could be in the coming year.

Indeed, vision moves us beyond our current reality into a better future where we might see a pile of wood, bricks, or stones as an architect envisions a home. Where we might see a boulder as a sculptor has visions of a beautiful sculpture. For a person or group with vision, current reality is merely the launching point of an exciting future.

This book begins with a process to see the present more clearly—to look closely at your community's strengths, challenges, and core values. *Stepping Forward Together* presents a wide array of data-gathering techniques (focus groups, surveys, interviews, assessments) for you to describe and diagnose your situation. It convenes honest conversations that may lift up some tough issues. Listing challenges, however, is not enough. The book argues that we need a hopeful, forward-looking vision of the future.

The book tells the familiar story of the biblical spies who were tasked to gather information about the Promised Land. When they came back from their reconnaissance mission, they did not recommend that the people go into the Promised Land. They thought the obstacles they faced provided too much resistance. Even though God had recently parted the Red Sea for them, they could not believe that God could overcome the obstacles in the road ahead. They thus looked at the future and were immobilized by fear.

The author contrasts the reluctance of the spies with the bold leadership of Joshua. When Joshua surveys the land, he gathers data but has faith that the future is in the Promised Land, not back in Egypt. He wants to be clay in God's hands. After the forty years of wandering, Moses passes the mantle of leadership to Joshua. At the edge of the Jordan River, Joshua places the Ark of the Covenant at the front of his procession. When the priest's feet enter the Jordan, the river splits. From this we learn that shared mission and vison can help people overcome resistance to change and help people *Step Forward Together.* This book has the hope that if we do the planning steps in good faith, God will bless our work.

This book asks you to take a leap of imagination to envision a different future. At every step along the way there are texts from our tradition to inspire and comfort you, reminding you that every generation of Jews has faced a challenging reality, dreamed of a better future, and then realized it, sometimes against tremendous odds.

Stepping Forward Together is not only about a vision process. It's also about a community-building group process. It's about bringing partners together—clergy, professional staff, and lay leaders—to increase the number of lenses by which we see current reality and to bring many minds and souls to the task of forming a vision and making change. Step by step, this book will allow you not only to form a new vision but also to grow closer in connection and partnership through that process. Whether you do a retreat or a full strategic plan, it will help your community become invested in the vision you wish to realize.

The author argues that this process is not just "Suggestion Box Judaism." The planning process goal is not simply to make long laundry lists of things others should do. The process invites new ideas but also looks for the people to drive them. In order to grow, the congregation needs to plan the increased capacity to implement it. This process is designed to generate new leadership. It also teaches important foundational leadership skills (data gathering, visioning, job definition, goal setting, etc.).

You will identify leaders who are passionate about this new vision and develop their leadership skills in listening, seeing, and acting to realize it.

We should note that ultimately this is a book about change, and all change involves loss.

Some commentators have suggested that some of the spies had made their living as herdsmen. When they heard the land was flowing with milk and honey, some may have feared that the importance of farming might soon surpass that of herding. Change offers opportunities. It can also raise fear of loss.

You and your community may need to leave behind strongly held assumptions about "how things are and always will be." You may discover things your community needs to stop doing, saying goodbye to long-treasured programs. Some people may even decide the new vision isn't for them and feel they must go elsewhere. All real change involves some measure of risk.

Leadership is not just about vision; it is also about bringing people on that journey and helping them manage the grief and sadness that accompany any worthwhile vision. As you lead the process, make space to process those feelings through study and reflection. Help people care for one another along the way.

Finally, this book is about optimism. In Judaism we have a beautiful tradition I call the "haftarah rule." Each week we read a Torah portion and also a portion with a similar theme from the prophets—our earliest "visionaries"—that we call the haftarah. When the rabbis chose those portions, they edited carefully to be sure that even when the prophet is offering criticism of the behavior of the people, each haftarah ends on a note of hope, promise, and optimism. Sometimes we even skip to a different passage or go back and repeat a verse from earlier in the haftarah to ensure that we end on a positive note. It's a reminder that, whatever their official role or title, good leaders are always COOs: chief optimism officers. Don't let your team give up. Help them see the current reality as clearly as possible—and then guide and encourage them as they form a bold vision for the future.

As you move through this book's process and activities, may you go *mihayil l'hayil*—from strength to strength!

Preface

Stepping Forward Together is a book about the power of hope to unleash congregational energy. It gives congregational leaders the tools they need to create a planning team and focus them on a hopeful, optimistic future. When leaders step forward to address the important issues of the community, their questions and conversations change that community. New leadership increases the *capacity* for ongoing conversations and community building. Just as our biblical hero Joshua demonstrated gifted leadership as he led the people into the Promised Land, so too his leadership brought out the gifts in his people as they entered the Promised Land together.

New Wisdom and Experience

This book is based on my previous book, *Stepping Forward*. That book was developed sixteen years ago when I was at the start of my consulting career. It was based on knowledge about change management that I had learned from my colleagues at the Alban Institute. The first seven chapters of this book build on that body of knowledge and include knowledge gained from an additional fifteen years of synagogue work with Alban and with my colleagues at United Synagogue of Conservative Judaism (USCJ).

Chapters 7 through 18 provide a detailed how-to manual for congregational planning leaders and facilitators. These annotated guides have been field tested in over sixty congregational planning projects. We have been able to use our USCJ consulting department as a "practice field." Through trial and error, we have refined these exercises to make sure that an average synagogue planning team would be able to use them successfully without the help of a paid consultant for the entire process. That was our goal. This book is the product of these efforts and they inspired the decision to write a revised edition of *Stepping Forward Together*.

This book is not for pundits. I avoid taking positions on the controversial issues of the day (America's polarized politics, Israel's policies, interfaith marriage, and so forth). This is a book of enduring leadership practices for planning practitioners.

Guiding Star

In welcoming readers to this planning journey, I have taken one of my core beliefs and put it to work in this book. I believe that leaders need to take the energy inside them and inspire others. My father told me the story of how when he was driving to Toledo, Ohio, on a sales call he got the inspiration for a new synagogue building in our little Midwestern town of Springfield, Ohio. When he got home, he got out his yellow legal pad that he kept by his bed to capture big sales ideas. He started drawing his dream building. He went on to lead the synagogue's building committee, and with his brother Fred, who was president, they helped the community make it happen. He believed in the power of a dream to inspire action.

Values in Action

When I talk to lay leaders today, I talk about their responsibility to take some of the energy they have and put it onto the shoulders of their fellow leaders. I have tried to put this value into action in *Stepping Forward Together*. In the first third of the book, you will learn about the forces that create energy in synagogues and those that diminish it. In the remainder of the book, you will see a sequence of visioning and planning exercises that will help planning leaders take the wisdom and energy they have and bring it to the board, task forces, and community. *Stepping Forward Together* is about the courage of the individual who dares to step forward. It is also about a process that brings hope and courage to others. Welcome to the journey.

Introduction
The Leadership Seder

And it shall be, when he sits on the throne of kingship, that he shall write for himself a copy of the teachings in a book before the levitical priests. And it shall be with him and he shall read it in all the days of his life, so that he may learn to fear the LORD his God, to keep all of the words of his teaching and these statutes.

—Deuteronomy 17:18–19

Stepping Forward Together argues that like the biblical kings, leaders must regularly revisit their mission, vision, values, and purpose. They must "step forward" and write a scroll for their leadership, for their generation, for their moment. The tradition argues that leaders should continuously strive to connect to God's will so they can step forward together.

Leaders Step Forward

Stepping Forward Together explains the stepping stones of synagogue visioning and planning. Leaders are tasked to plan the agenda of the board. They need a plan to develop leaders. They need to create long-term plans to sustain the synagogue. Whatever the scope of their planning, they will need to learn to look at issues from multiple angles and consider multiple paths.

Some leaders may say, "We all know what we do here. We have services, we do life cycle events, we celebrate the holidays, we have a school. What more needs to be said?" Some congregational leaders have a very strong sense of their culture, their context, and their purpose. Nonetheless, most will find it helpful to reflect on how the congregation makes the connection between ancient truths and current realities. This effort is like the writing of a new congregational scroll—a forward-looking plan for the future.

Reluctant versus Courageous Leaders

In a well-known biblical story, Moses sends out twelve spies to scout out the Promised Land. All but two (Joshua and Caleb) return with the report that while the land is flowing with milk and honey, the Israelites would face enormous challenges because "the people who inhabit the country are powerful, and the cities are fortified and very large" (Numbers 13:28). They report that the country they "traversed and scouted is one that devours its settlers" (Numbers 13:32). The spies were fearful and reluctant leaders, feeling like grasshoppers as they looked at their adversaries and contemplated the future.

Moses had asked the spies to bring back some of the fruit of the new land to share their experience of joy that the land offered. Instead they gave a report that frightened the people. They were afraid to step forward.

One might argue that to proceed into the land without adequate information would have been reckless. Moses instructed them to gather data. When they considered the data, their conclusions, however, were negative. The text seems to indicate that God felt that the spies lacked faith in God's promise and only highlighted the challenges of the road ahead. God had promised them that they would prosper and now they were doubting that promise.

Joshua Steps Up and Scatters His Enemies

Contrast the leadership of the spies with Joshua's leadership as he led the people to step forward and cross the Jordan to enter Canaan, the Promised Land. We are told that when Joshua and the priests enter the river with the Ark of the Covenant, it miraculously separates the waters of the Jordan, recreating the Red Sea miracle. Joshua's procession is blessed because the priests walk at the front carrying the Ark. We reenact this every week during Shabbat services when the Torah is brought out from the Ark in the synagogue.

When the ark would set out Moses would say:

Advance O Lord!
May your enemies be scattered,
And may your foes flee before you!
(Numbers 10:35)

Joshua is able to part the waters of resistance because his mission is for the sake of heaven, not for his own self-interest. In order to promote their mission with passion, leaders need to have the hands-on immersive experience of writing their own scroll, their own plan. As you see in the frontispiece illustration, *Stepping Forward Together* takes its title from the moment when Joshua and the priests step into the waters of the Jordan. Throughout the tradition we find both those who are reluctant and those who are willing to step in and step forward. This book is dedicated to those who have the courage to step forward.

This book provides tools for leadership development and for an in-depth planning process called synagogue visioning and planning (SVP). Using this book, you will be able to consider your values and practices and engage your team with the challenge of building a covenantal community. You will learn new leadership rituals that will guide you along the stepping stones to accomplish your synagogue's plan.

The Leadership Seder: Telling the Story

How can leaders ritualize their leadership journey? Jewish tradition mandates that we tell the story of the Exodus from Egypt *every* year at our Passover seders. Our tradition challenges us to remember and to experience what it was like to be a slave, and the seder itself is designed to help us feel as if we were actually there, as if we ourselves experienced that bondage. Leadership development programs can learn a great deal from the Passover seder. It is a showcase of experiential learning. There is something for everyone: prayers to read, texts to listen to, objects to touch, things to smell and taste, songs to sing and hear. We are challenged to engage all of our senses and to include all types of learners.

The Haggadah (from "*lehagid*" meaning "to tell") is the book that guides us through the Passover seder, like a facilitator's guide to help us teach the stories and the rituals of the holiday. We hope that this book will be your Haggadah, your facilitator's guide to the planning process, a guide that you can turn to again and again and find new insights each time.

Like any new ritual, it will take extra energy to bring people to the planning table. Just as the seder has its narrative and its cast of characters, so we will revisit several well-known biblical narratives to help us tell our leadership story.

Our Haggadah: A Leadership Guide

I. Thriving Synagogues and Their Leaders

In part I we lift up the role of the synagogue in a time when it is under pressure from powerful, disruptive forces and besieged by doubts from members, staff, and national observers. We look at the attributes of a thriving synagogue and ask leaders to explore how they could build on their strengths. We then look at thriving synagogue leadership and explore some of the things that help leaders step forward in challenging times.

Key Questions

How do we make the case for the compelling value of our synagogues in a world that questions these types of legacy institutions? How do we develop a shared vocabulary about what makes a thriving and sustainable synagogue? How do we become positive leaders who can build on the strengths of the congregation and the talents of its leaders? How do we engage in reflection on the challenges we face without losing hope?

II. Understanding the Lay of the Land

Part II of the book looks at the challenges of synagogue planning in the current environment. We look at the disruptive forces impacting the synagogue as well as some of the opportunities that are presented by these changes. We look at how planners define the scope of planning they want to embrace. We look at a congregation's readiness for change. We review the importance of maintaining momentum in planning and map out the steps in the campaign of change.

Key Questions

How do we get agreement on key facts about the congregation and its context? How do we explore different approaches to planning? How much capacity for change is there? Given the challenges of the work, how do we gauge the congregation's readiness for change? How do leaders manage the campaign of change and maintain momentum to finish the plan?

III. Getting Organized for the Journey

Part III is an updated presentation of SVP. At USCJ we call this Sulam for Strategic Planners (SSP). SSP provides a guide to help congregations take manageable planning steps within their capacity. We discuss how to create the planning team, which we call the steering committee. We describe key subcommittees (teams) of the steering committee that work on mission/vision, communications, and data gathering. We go into detail about the challenges of gathering and making meaning from the data. We look at various tools for data collection such as interviews, community conversations, and surveys.

Key Questions

How do we design the composition of our planning committee? Who should we recruit? What do planning leaders expect from fellow planners? What should prospective committee members expect from planning leaders? What kinds of data should planners gather? How do we welcome the stories of our members? How do we gain insights into their wants and needs?

IV. Making Meaning of Information

Part IV is about the process of engaging the steering committee, the board, the staff, and the congregation in making meaning from the data they have gathered through various planning workshops. How do we create a hopeful, forward-looking vision for the future? This will lead to the development of strategies and goals for various focus areas of the synagogue and will also provide strategic direction for task forces.

Key Questions

How do we create a hopeful, forward-looking vision for the future? How do we provide strategic direction to our task forces? How do we orient and engage new planners as they join the committee in the task force phase?

V. Lessons Learned

Part V reviews the process of report writing, plan adoption, and implementation. It also explores the lessons we've learned from our strategic planning work and from developing strategic leaders.

The Synagogue Visioning and Planning Journey

I come from an entrepreneurial family. My grandfather was entrepreneurial enough to leave Russia, get on a boat, and come to America, and my father started a cleaning products business with a few employees and saw it grow into a major business. I had a chance to reflect on this family history when I taught marketing at the University of Dayton. One of the definitions of an entrepreneur is one who steps forward. Encouraging leaders to step forward was the passion that motivated me to write this book. I hope it stirs up your energy to step forward as well.

This book is for planning committees, leadership development teams, and boards. These are the people who have been challenged to make the connections between our ancient traditions and our current challenges. As they make these connections, they will help others learn to make them as well.

The Visioning and Planning Team

The SVP process is led by a steering committee of ten to twelve people, including the senior rabbi and the executive director, if there is one. Other staff and clergy may be added where appropriate. The steering committee meets at least monthly for about a year to gather data, recruit participants, conduct workshops, and debrief individual experiences. The steering committee is composed of core leaders of the board, such as the past president and committee chairs, and it is seasoned with fresh leaders who have demonstrated spiritual maturity, have planning skills, and have shown a commitment to Jewish life in the community, if not on the synagogue board. Steering committee members recruit various segments (such as new members, longstanding members, worship-focused members, empty nesters) of the congregation to participate in guided group interviews, which we call community conversations. The steering committee, the professional staff, and additional stakeholders representing different groups go through various planning exercises over the course of the year.

Clergy and Staff

This book is also for rabbis and other clergy and staff who want to encourage leaders to jump into the waters of new learning. They want to help create a framework to discuss what matters. SVP rabbis believe that in order to part the sea of resistance and inertia, they need to allow the free flow of feedback from community conversation meetings and planning workshops. They figuratively "set up more chairs" at the community conversation table and welcome new leaders to join the discussion. They welcome this new energy and strive to be open to hearing ideas and suggestions, even if they do not always fit their assumptions.

SVP rabbis learn not to be reactive. Just because members provide input about what they would like the congregation to do does not mean the congregation is required to act on every suggestion. SVP rabbis are optimistic that as key members of the steering committee, they can help shape the leadership conversation. They can listen with empathy and develop a plan that connects the will of members to the will of God. They can be what educator Parker Palmer calls "connectors and weavers."

Even if they are not always in authority in the process, these rabbis feel comfortable that they can be appreciated as an authority. Like Bezalel, the master craftsman of the biblical tabernacle, SVP rabbis appreciate and welcome the unique contributions and gifts of each member. They help put those gifts together.

At USCJ, we require the senior rabbi of a congregation to be on the steering committee. Planners need the rabbi's guidance and rabbis need the deep leadership learning that planning provides. They are encouraged to ensure that senior staff are involved in the data-gathering and task force stage. In different cultures, other clergy and staff may join the steering committee as leaders see best.

Lay Leaders

SVP is also for lay leaders who want to expand the size of their core leadership and understand the importance of investing in the development of new leaders. These lay leaders want to find a way to integrate new and seasoned leaders by enabling them to work together on an engaging and important project. They believe that by developing shared facts, shared values, shared goals, and shared accountability, they will build the kind of team that breaks through the forces of resistance and helps the congregation step forward. They know that the rabbi and other clergy are particularly well positioned to help them understand how the tradition informs this journey. They are open to sharing their thoughts and reflections with the rabbi and staff. They understand that the process of dialogue can be as important as the final plan. They hope to develop their capacity for strategic thinking and collaborative planning. While plans may become outdated, the capacity to think strategically will be a foundational and life-long skill critical for dealing with a rapidly changing world.

Executive Directors

SVP calls on the leadership expertise of executive directors, who help with recruitment and logistics as well as data gathering. They help anticipate administrative barriers to success and identify volunteer talents and build relationships. They can also help look for opportunities to put some of the creative ideas on a fast track. Executive directors can also help ensure that important documents are treated with respect and distributed. They support the work of the chairs at every stage and help drive the planning process.

Who Else Goes on the Journey?

SVP requires leaders to recruit a steering committee and four to seven task forces. Task forces can address such topics as new members, long-standing members, families with young children, empty nesters, etc., or key areas of synagogue life such as leadership, finance, education, ritual, and social justice.

Synagogue leaders are sometimes surprised by the level of commitment we require for SVP. "You want our steering committee of twelve to recruit twenty-five to fifty additional planners? How can we do that?" As consultants, we know that if leaders aim too high, the goal will seem unattainable. If they aim too low, there will be no urgency. We don't expect leaders to leap tall buildings in a single bound, but we do ask them to stretch and build their skills. Recruiting volunteers is a foundational skill that SVP helps to strengthen.

The Power of Large Groups

One complaint we have heard over the years of working with synagogues is that the mission, vision, and strategies developed by long-range planning committees were not implemented or anchored in the culture. Too often the documents are left in a binder in the synagogue office to gather dust. In most cases, that was a result of having small planning groups that did not have the critical mass to change the leadership or the congregational culture.

Research has shown that "the fate of the congregation is intertwined with the percentage of its members who choose to be actively involved. The high correlation suggests that a change in the size of the active core *ipso facto* changes the nature of the congregation" (Sales 2006, 3). By including a high participation requirement in the SVP design, we encourage congregations to increase their overall capacity for leadership, which will produce longer lasting benefits.

Our tradition lifts up the importance of gathering large leadership groups. We like the number seventy, which in Jewish tradition represents a complete community. Jacob moved his family of seventy to Egypt, and it was this group that would lay the foundation for the Israelite nation. When Moses traveled up the mountain to accept the Torah, he brought seventy leaders with him to the foot of the mountain. The Sanhedrin, the ancient rabbinic court, had seventy members. We invite a large group of leaders (from approximately thirty-five to seventy) to join this effort because a critical mass of leaders will be less likely to leave the plan on the shelf and more likely to move forward with implementation.

> SVP is about people, not just paper! It doesn't just create documents; it calls forward the gifts of the membership.

What Does the Journey Look Like?

Joshua knew that the steps along the journey needed to be commemorated. That is why when he entered the land of Canaan, he took the stones from the Jordan and built a monument on the other side of the river.

Here are some of the key stepping stones for SVP:

- Steering Committee Start Up—Mission Discussion
- SWOT Analysis
- Launch Congregational Survey
- Start Community Conversations
- Data Debrief: Explore Emerging Themes from Data
- Vision Builder Exercise: Create Vision for Focus Areas
- Launch of Task Forces: Welcome More Planners
- Task Force Phase: Create Task Force Report and Recommendation
- Town Meetings: Welcome Questions and Comments
- Priority Setting Workshop: Look for Initiatives with Impact
- Writing Phase: Write Report
- Board Approval and Implementation

Our process normally requires a month or two of pre-planning and about three months of data gathering, followed by data analysis and an executive summary. We then do the Vision Builder Workshop and the Task Force Start Up. This is followed by two to three months of task force work, and then a Priority Setting Workshop. It takes about twelve months to complete all the steps and then a couple of months to write the plan and get it approved by the board.

Deliverables

As consultants leading this process, we ask that our congregations complete the following "deliverables":

1. Fact Book, Thriving Congregation Assessment and Committee Interviews
2. Situation and SWOT Analysis
3. Congregational Survey
4. Community Conversations
5. Emerging Themes from Survey, Conversations, Interviews, and Thriving Congregations Assessment
6. Congregational Vision Statement
7. Strategic Direction for Task Forces
8. Priority Recommendations from Task Forces
9. Final Report
10. Board Adoption and Implementation Plan

Is SVP Only for Synagogues?

The SVP model was designed for synagogues, and our case studies and examples are drawn from that environment. We believe that these tools can also be helpful to Jewish community centers, Jewish Federation teams, camp boards, other Jewish agencies, and nonprofits.

There are certainly insights and tools here that can be adapted for churches. You would just need to make some translations and build some bridges from our context to yours. I hope that you will find joy in learning how one faith tradition can inform and raise useful questions for another. I hope that whatever part of this journey you embrace, it will be encouraging and productive—an inspired journey of hope and heart.

As we begin this *Stepping Forward* journey together, let's begin with the Traveler's Prayer (*Tefilat HaDerekh*):

May it be Your will, Lord our God and God of our ancestors, to guide us in peace and sustain us in peace, to lead us to our desired destination in health and joy and peace. . . . Save us from every enemy and disaster on the way, and from all calamities. . . . Bless the work of our hands. May we find grace, love, and compassion in Your sight and in the sight of all who see us. . . . Praised are You, Lord, who hears prayer.

PART I

Thriving Synagogues and Their Leaders

Chapter 1
Thriving Congregations
Building on Strengths

Synagogue visioning and planning (SVP) is a process that increases the capacity of synagogue leaders to *think strategically and to act courageously*. Planners need to understand the challenges of a changing world. They need a hopeful, forward-looking vision and a step-by-step process to lead their communities through a campaign of change.

In our work at United Synagogue our Sulam leadership team has developed some insights about *what helps congregations to thrive*. Leaders come from many backgrounds. It is helpful if they have a shared vocabulary about what synagogue health and vitality looks like. The Thriving Congregations Assessment (TCA) provides a vocabulary to help leaders consider synagogue strategies together. We will also demonstrate how you can use the assessment process to build on some of your congregation's strengths. Doing so can create a ripple effect that will spur other positive changes.

In approaching this work we believe leaders can develop insights from our ancient texts, from fellow leaders, and from our network of congregations. When we get to tough issues, we are bolstered by the knowledge that we are not the first Jewish leaders who have wrestled with the challenges of our day. We can stand taller because we know we are not alone. We draw upon ancient wells of wisdom as we address contemporary problems. Let's reflect on the following text:

Rabbi Hanina: Torah is like a deep well full of water whose waters were cold and sweet and delicious, but no one was able to drink from it. Then a certain person came along, and supplied the well with one cord tied to another, one rope tied to another, and drew water out of the well, and drank from it. Then everyone began to draw water and drink it. (Shir HaShirim Rabbah 1.1:8)

15

In this story, there was a deep well of sweet water, but the people, using their normal methods, could not access it. A leader came forward who found some innovative way to reach what had been unreachable. First, he recognized the assets all around him. He saw the short cord, the long cord, the thick cord, and the somewhat frayed cord. Next, he brought the different elements together and repurposed them in order to create a longer cord. As you will see, our planning process celebrates the leaders who step forward and help the community build capacity.

Keystone Habits at Alcoa

In the book *The Power of Habit*, author Charles Duhigg tells the story of Alcoa Aluminum. Alcoa had been struggling. They hired a new CEO named Paul O'Neill. When O'Neill was introduced to investors, he didn't choose to focus his talk on profit margins, revenue projections, or anything else that would normally be comforting to Wall Street ears. He began, "I want to talk to you about worker safety." The room went silent. It was reported that investors ran out of the room as soon as the presentation was finished. One analyst sprinted to a pay phone and called his twenty largest clients. He said, "The board put a crazy hippie in charge, and he's going to kill the company." The investor told Duhigg, "I ordered them to sell their stock immediately."

Why did O'Neill focus on safety? Alcoa had experienced terrible labor-management relationships. He needed to find a place to start where there was some common ground. He chose safety because the union cared about worker safety, and management wanted to reduce costs, injuries, and lost work time. It was potentially a win-win issue they could build on.

When management and labor worked together to strengthen this one area, they found they could bring energy to other areas of the company. In this way the "cord for the bucket" got longer. They could reach deeper agreement about a range of best practices.

The larger lesson for a synagogue planner is that by focusing on a few critical issues, or what Duhigg refers to as "keystone habits," you may be able to create some changes that ripple through the entire culture. "It turns out that focusing on one, highly impactful habit can improve several routines—and the bottom line," said Paul O'Neill. Profits at Alcoa dramatically improved in the following year.

In SVP we don't tell the leadership what task forces to create. We may feel strongly that they need to work on something, but we need to let them work on the things they have the energy and the capacity to do. As in the Alcoa case, they may have energy for something like worker safety that on the surface may seem odd but might just be the thing to bring people together and create energy. The consultant may see something else that is critical, but the congregation may lack the capacity to do it. As consultants and facilitators, we can't want something more than the congregational leaders want it for themselves. They need to find their own strengths and build on them: "to lengthen the cord."

The Thriving Congregations Assessment: A Leadership Engagement Tool

We at USCJ created the Thriving Congregations Framework and Assessment primarily as a tool for the meaningful engagement of synagogue leadership. It is meant to help the leaders around the table reflect on their situation and make the connections between their different leadership perspectives and experiences. When leaders are empowered with a shared language, they are more able to bring their diverse gifts to the board table. Working together, they can make a longer cord and find new solutions.

Many of our congregations come from a view of scarcity. They feel they have to compete for scarce resources rather than collaborate to make what they have reach farther. They may set groups within the congregation against each other: old versus young, new versus longstanding members, ritual conservatives versus liberals, etc. They may become competitive with other institutions in the community. We believe that if we can uncover some of their assets, aspects that are currently thriving, we can unleash new energy. We can build a sense of capacity so that more people can get their needs met.

The Roots of the Assessment

I have been working extensively with congregations since 2001 and have worked with over five hundred congregations at one time or another as a consultant for the Alban Institute. This assessment draws from my work at the Alban Institute, as well as from my work with UJA Federation of New York and change management processes like Synagogue 2000 (captured in the book *Sacred Strategies*). This model was also discussed in an article coauthored by Dr. David Kiel in *Practicing Social Change: Renewing Jewish Congregational Life Using Blended OD Methods, A Report from the Frontline of Community Engagement.* This chapter reflects some of the input from colleagues of the National Training Labs community.

The Thriving Congregations Assessment is also rooted in my experience at United Synagogue. As we developed our Sulam leadership programs, our team has been exploring how to help strengthen synagogues to be more successful and to build their capacity. Our connection to the stories of our approximately six hundred USCJ-affiliated congregations is one of the critical advantages we have in developing new approaches. USCJ strives to be a learning organization. Our synagogues offer us countless opportunities for experimentation and innovation. We have the capacity to convene congregational leaders, gather data, and explore ways to shape our leadership work together.

The Thriving Congregations Framework and Assessment allows the assessment, as a diagnostic tool, to identify areas that are thriving and those that need development. We use the assessment to find areas of strength that we can build on to create a positive vision for the congregation's future. The TCA is intended to do the following:

- Identify areas where the congregation is currently thriving and explore what is driving growth.
- Identify areas where the congregation feels stuck and explore what is getting in the way.
- Consider unexplored areas where a congregation could potentially thrive.
- Connect leaders to ideas, resources, and partners that will help them thrive.

The TCA is a great dialogic tool. It has the potential to change the conversation from focusing on what is wrong to focusing on what is thriving and how to build on those thriving elements.

The Thriving Congregations Assessment Leads to Deeper Reflection

Congregations are complex. While there is no single "recipe" for a thriving congregation, we do believe that there are some ingredients that are usually present when a thriving congregation is at work. We call these elements the attributes of a thriving congregation.

We ask the executive committee, and then the board and senior staff, to take the assessment so that they can collaborate and reflect on the results. One person's insight is not enough. The TCA is a way to invite leaders to join together to go deeper in reflection so they can attain new insights.

Leadership with Energy, Growth, and Momentum

According to our data, the rabbi is one of the most important reasons why people remain members. The rabbi is critical in casting a vision and aligning the rest of the organization to that vision. With that said, we do not just look at the star qualities or personal charisma (star power) of the clergy. We don't assess their ability to give a great sermon or chant a prayer. We don't focus on their ability to remember everyone's name at Kiddush lunch, as valuable as these skills may be. The assessment looks at how their skilled leadership is motivating more people to grow Jewishly or more capable leaders to step up. Do they bring people together to learn something—to "lengthen the cord"?

Leaders Continuously Strive to Improve

Because no two congregations are alike, we do not suggest that you try to graft the programs of another congregation onto yours without thinking about how they will fit in your culture. What might be considered a very successful program in one congregation might fail elsewhere because they lack the same staff, volunteer capacity, or demographics.

It is important for thriving congregations to understand the following principles:

- No congregations are thriving in all areas. Thriving congregations do not have to excel in everything.
- A complete failure of one of these foundational practice areas, however, can take an otherwise thriving congregation off track. Poor organizational structure or lack of lay or staff accountability, for example, can frustrate the best intended plans.
- There is no one "right" place to start. Leaders can focus on the development of a foundational practice in one area and find that it provides new insight and energy for another. For example, a commitment to collaboration can help leaders be more open to outside resources and partners. This might lead to working with new coalition partners on social justice issues.
- Leaders can, and must, strive to continually strengthen and address these attributes in order to thrive.

Foundational Practices for Kehillot

We have repurposed the concept of Duhigg's "keystone habits" and now call them "foundational practices." We believe that leaders can increase the vitality of their congregations by focusing on these practices and learning to develop attributes of thriving congregations.

Each of the seven practices is further defined by two or more "attributes." An attribute is an observable practice. An attribute's presence connotes a strength, and its absence suggests a direction for improvement. We have identified twenty-two attributes of thriving congregations.

I have truncated the descriptions of these attributes. The complete TCA assessment can be found in appendix resource 1.

Thriving Congregations Assessment Practices and Attributes

Foundational Principle	To what degree does your congregation have . . .
Develop a shared compelling vision of purposeful Jewish living	• a participative planning process; • clergy that is trusted, stable, and visionary; • a commitment to continuous improvement; and • a clear plan for communicating the vision to the congregation?
Engage in reflective and accountable leadership	• clear job descriptions and reporting lines; • internal and external assessments; and • a process and method for developing new leadership?
Manage change and conflict	• an innovative strategic plan; • leaders who are willing to take risks to bring about needed changes; and • leaders who have the capacity to manage conflicts and disagreements?

Ensure sustainable and sound operations	• leaders who are committed to transparency in goal setting and decision making and in operations and finances; and • written policies and plans for sustainable financial management, membership development, and administrative operations?
Welcome participation and connection	• a stated commitment to inclusion; • affinity groups for different segmeths of the congregation; • processes to recognize and support members in times of transition; and • special programs for children and teens?
Motivate deeper engagement in Torah and Tefila	• programs about Jewish history, culture, and practice; • ongoing groups to support spiritual and ritual involvement; and • initiatives that connect tradition and ritual to social justice work?
Advocate for prophetic justice and practice Covenantal Caring	• activities that deepen connections to Israel; • opportunities for people with different abilities and needs to participate in all aspects of the congregation; and • ways of advocating for social justice in the community, in Israel, and around the world?

Note on exercise: Leaders can score their congregations on the TCA instrument in about five to seven minutes during a workshop. They rate how much of each attribute they currently exhibit (a great deal, some, a little, or not at all). They then are asked to identify one strength they can build on. They may also choose to identify an area where they would like to do better, or "hope to thrive." We have used this form with synagogue presidents for an initial discussion. We also use this assessment with strategic planning teams. TCA has empowered congregational leaders to develop a shared vocabulary to describe a healthy congregation and helped leaders maintain hope by focusing on what is thriving and how to build on it, rather than focusing on what is wrong.

Conclusion

Judaism is about a constant striving for growth. It challenges the modern Jewish mind to wrestle with the richness of the tradition while repurposing and reengaging with it. Our United Synagogue Sulam leadership programs (strategic planning, board development, leadership development) were inspired by this challenge. We encourage leaders to reach up for the next rung on the ladder (Sulam)—to grow. We are hopeful that the TCA will engage leaders in reflective leadership and motivate them to develop a compelling vision of purposeful Jewish living and develop strategies that can inspire greater learning, spirituality, engagement, and acts of kindness.

Exercise

Please take five to seven minutes to take the TCA in your appendix: resource 1.

Identify three things that are thriving now.

Pick one and explore how you might build on it.

Pick one area that needs some further development.

Chapter 2
Building a Thriving Leadership Community

We discussed our Thriving Congregations Assessment in chapter 1. In 2016 we used the assessment to study twenty of our largest and best resourced congregations. These large congregations scored high on their commitment to Israel, on being caring and inclusive, on commitment to social justice, and on providing engaging learning experiences, but they were underdeveloped in several leadership areas:

- Congregations lacked a shared vision and a communication plan to get their message across.
- Leaders did not have clear expectations of their boards and committees and ways to hold them accountable.
- There was no leadership pipeline or formal process to develop leaders.
- There were few written strategies and goals that would provide strategic focus.
- Leaders could not articulate a financial plan that would educate the community on what it took to sustain the community.

We will argue that synagogue visioning and planning can improve many of these leadership practices and functions as an advanced form of leadership development.

The following twelve principles are designed to help leadership communities (rabbis, professional staff, board members, and volunteers) to thrive.

1. Leaders Share a Vocabulary of Success

Most of my clients know I was a business executive before I was a congregational consultant, so when I arrive at a synagogue to lead a workshop, it is not uncommon for the treasurer to corner me in the hall and say, "Thank God you're here. I've been trying to convince this group that the synagogue needs to be run like a business, and I know you understand how important business is." Later on in the workshop, this same treasurer often appears crestfallen when I announce that the synagogue is not, in fact, something that can be run solely as a business.

> I believe that if members try to bring their briefcase straight from the office, they will not create a plan that allows the congregation to step forward together.

Jim Collins writes, "We need to reject the naïve imposition of the language of business on the social sectors and instead jointly embrace the language of greatness" (2005, 2). The congregation's leaders need a strategic map, but it doesn't come from just one of the professional disciplines around the table. We need a collective map shared by all leaders, like the Thriving Congregations Framework in chapter 1, to provide a vocabulary about what helps congregations thrive.

2. Leaders Connect to a Compelling Sacred Purpose

Many churches see their leaders as disciples. These are people with extraordinary commitment and passion. Disciples are more than their secular portfolios. Synagogue leaders likewise need to strive to be more than the lawyers, accountants, or social workers on the board. They need to be able to connect sacred texts to real-life situations, inviting spiritual reflections, taking a moment for prayer in an afternoon workshop, or connecting their work with an upcoming holiday. How do you attract new members? You introduce them to role models, leaders who love Jewish living and leading.

Welcome Leaders to Step Up

At a mega church I visited, the senior pastor explained that his Wednesday youth program had forty volunteer mentors who had been trained in his lay ministry program to work with teenage youth. Each mentor also had a recent high school grad who helped him work with the group of eight kids. "What keeps the senior pastor up at night?" I asked. He said his focus was on supporting these "spiritually gifted" lay mentors and finding the next generation of mentors. He told me he had found the head of this youth ministry working in a grocery warehouse. The senior pastor saw his spiritual leadership potential and trained him in their youth ministry curriculum.

The pastor is always on the lookout for leadership gifts. He is hoping to find those who feel called to serve. I challenge synagogue leaders to be creative in looking for talent and recruiting gifted lay leaders. The pastor found his man in a grocery warehouse.

SVP CASE

According to Irwin Kula, rabbi and president of the National Jewish Center for Learning and Leadership, leaders likewise need to be able to see the sacred in new places. You can see the sacred in how leaders support the staff or give each other loving feedback for the sake of the community. You can see the sacred when people give financial gifts that are beyond what is expected. You can see the sacred when people struggle to learn new things—even when it's a little embarrassing. The sacred is not just in the siddur; it is on the walls of the workshop sessions and in the circles of community conversations. It is in the notes that debrief the steering committee meetings and on the walls of the synagogue foyer, celebrating the work of students or honoring a volunteer.

SVP gathers a diverse group of people with different skills and engages them in a process that ritualizes their work as a sacred set of steps and inspires them to discover the sacred all around the community.

3. Leadership "Stirs the Pot"

Dr. Gil Rendle encourages leaders to make a careful assessment of their environment when they embark on change (Rendle 1998). He tries to help them understand how congregations naturally resist change and how to help people be less reluctant about change. Congregational learning requires leaders who will "stir the pot" and stimulate a leadership conversation. I said stir, not heat the pot up so much it boils over the top. Leaders need to get buy-in for some pot stirring and get permission for some experiments.

Most members, however, expect the leaders to maintain the status quo. If leaders do not do this, they may be attacked or replaced. The normal congregational system is in some kind of equilibrium. Change leaders who "stir the pot" can certainly make "managers and maintainers of the day to day" nervous.

The steps of the south entrance to the ancient Temple in Jerusalem were made uneven so that the people would not rush up the steps. They would approach the sacred carefully. SVP challenges leaders to explore change but suggests the "slow and steady" steps. Shortcuts can be hazardous to your health.

4. Leaders Tell the Truth: Make an Honest Assessment

A number of trends, factors, and forces are affecting Jewish life in general and synagogue life in particular. So an awareness of these trends, as well as the challenges and opportunities they represent, is essential for effective synagogue leadership. In the planning process, we ask leaders to create a fact book with critical congregational data. We suggest leaders explore surveys and focus groups (see the chapter on community conversations) to listen to peoples' stories about what is working well and what could be better. We need to gather quantitative and qualitative data. We can debate the implications of what we are learning later.

Later I will discuss the challenges of mobility, assimilation, the cost of Jewish living, the stresses of two-income households, intermarriage, and a general reluctance to commit to traditional organizations. These are some of the well-known forces that synagogue leaders discuss. What is mentioned less, however, is that the Jewish community has been extraordinarily successful. Jewish immigrants came to America for economic opportunity and political freedom. They have achieved both. Jews have prospered and gained respected positions in government, the professions, and business, and anti-Semitism has substantially declined in the sixty years since World War II.

In recent years, Jewish learning has expanded exponentially. Few major cities are without significant adult study opportunities, and anyone with an internet connection can quickly access a host of Jewish websites offering everything from commentaries on the week's Torah portion to essays on Jewish communal issues. During the COVID-19 crisis congregational learning expanded further as leaders developed new capacities to bring school materials, adult education, and ritual services online. This has given people ways to enrich their Jewish lives.

> Regardless of whether a trend is positive or negative, an asset or a liability, it needs to be understood and managed.

The biblical spies made a long list of what was wrong with the Promised Land. The opportunities of the land faded to the background. In the end their negativity immobilized them and they were afraid to step forward. SVP follows the data-gathering phase with a hopeful, forward-looking vision of the future. It challenges leaders to bring new energy to fix problems and creatively explore opportunities.

5. Leaders Put a Frame Around the Work: Help Make Meaning

My Dayton, Ohio, rabbi, Irving Bloom, said at his retirement ceremony that he had been blessed to be a "maker of frames." He told us that it had been his privilege to bear witness to moments of joy and sorrow and to put a frame around these moments so people could make meaning from them. One important leadership task is the ability to frame our leadership situation and help people make sense of it.

According to Lee Bolman and Terrence Deal in their book *Reframing Organizations* (2003, 15), organizations provide several frameworks for leaders: the structural, the human, the political, and the symbolic. In this book I will discuss situations that call on leaders to employ all of these frameworks.

When you design the steering committee and clarify its relationship with the board, you are using the "structural frame." When you look for the right mix of people and try to build them into the planning process, you are using the "human frame." When you recruit the key community stakeholders and help find some common ground, you are working in the "political frame." When you let members tell their stories in community conversations, you are emphasizing the "symbolic frame."

SVP gathers lots of information. Leaders have to learn to see the emerging themes and patterns in the data so that they can put a frame around it and make meaning from it (see my article "Seeing like Barnes"). SVP understands that not everyone was born a natural visionary leader, but many can gain a leadership perspective by learning to use different leadership frameworks.

6. Leaders Do Strategic Work

Although strategic thinking is not well developed in all leaders, this skill is critical in times of change. People may feel that they were not born leaders, but they can learn to be more strategic by doing strategic work. A successful planning model should simplify the process enough to ensure that the planning leaders can be successful in key strategic tasks.

- Chapter 7: Planning Committee Start Up
- Chapter 8: Gathering Data
- Chapter 12: Data Debrief
- Chapter 13: Creating a Hopeful Forward-Looking Vision
- Chapter 14: All Task Force Workshop
- Chapter 16: Priority-Setting Workshop

When planners review survey data, participate in focus groups, and develop emerging themes, they begin to see patterns. They can help teammates join them in reflection. This is strategic work.

While we argue that strategic thinking is important today, the history of strategic planning in congregations is mixed. It is not uncommon for congregations to do facility planning with a fundraising consultant in preparation for a capital campaign. In this case, planning is tied to a very concrete goal. It has a focus. But when congregations face changes in demographics, cultural changes, increased diversity, or generational changes, they are less likely to see these as requiring real commitment.

Elite and relatively small leadership teams have tried to streamline the process by limiting the involvement of other stakeholders. Sadly, many found that their plans were never implemented.

Judaism argues that we gain major insights about God, holiness, and righteousness by "doing" things. At Mount Sinai, the Jewish people answered God's challenge by saying, "All that the LORD has spoken we will faithfully do" (Exodus 24:7). We comprehend the abstract by doing the concrete—observing commandments. SVP helps leaders attain such qualities as vision, energy, collaboration, and accountability by doing SVP tasks.

7. Leaders Welcome Volunteers on the Practice Field

According to Malcolm S. Knowles (1973), adults need to apply their life experiences and professional expertise to their congregational work. Experts in training are well aware of how much information is lost even one day after a workshop. What sticks is what we integrate and practice. Mentors need to provide a "practice field" where volunteer mentees can bring their life experiences and talents to the leadership work.

Most volunteers step forward because they have experienced the effective leadership of another person. They did not respond to an ad; they responded out of admiration. The right person asked them. As explained in my article on the Valley Beth Shalom Counseling Center (2019), many health care professionals were invited to a planning meeting. At first no one stepped up. Then a certain psychiatrist stepped forward to offer his life wisdom, experience, and professional training. His commitment, vision, and energy led to the creation of a counseling center that has grown to over twenty volunteer counselors.

Successful leadership development processes often involve the creation of small groups in which individuals can get "hands-on" experiences with synagogue learning and deeds. Our SVP model starts by creating a healthy team environment, which we call "the container," for learning. It fosters the accountability of planners to each other and to the planning process. It then creates task forces to create new "practice fields" for others to engage in strategic work.

8. Leaders Build Collaborative and Supportive Teams

The Center for Creative Leadership calls teamwork "the most frequently valued managerial competence," and, according to John Seely Brown, head of Xerox's Research Park, "If you ask successful people, they will tell you that they learned the most from and with each other" (Goleman 1995, 202).

In 2019, USCJ and its partner organization, the North American Association of Synagogue Executives, studied teamwork in synagogues. We found the following underdeveloped areas: clear job descriptions, shared goals and strategies, and processes for teammates to disclose their needs and seek support from others.

The good news is that SVP can strengthen these team-building capacities. SVP encourages leaders to be reflective about their own strengths and maintain an openness and curiosity about the strengths of others. This kind of emotional intelligence is critical for thriving teams. In the

SVP process leaders work together in small groups for months; the process helps them build relationships and learn how groups can work to achieve important shared goals.

9. Leaders Ask for Help

Consultants and facilitators can be helpful in creating a sense of urgency by identifying areas of opportunity and concern. They can help maintain momentum and energy by helping leaders imagine a promising future. While the economics of synagogues do not ensure steady consulting work, it is my hope that this book encourages an array of people to take on roles as coaches, mentors, and consultants in their areas. Many denominational organizations offer forums where leaders can share ideas.

10. Leaders Expand the Leadership Community

One of the problems with some strategic planning efforts is that they may create a document that has little buy-in.

In an era of declining volunteerism, planning efforts need to create new energy and momentum. If only six people go into the boardroom and "knock the plan out," who will implement it? How will this work engage new leadership prospects?

Effective leadership development and change management will require the engagement of a wide array of current and potential leadership to build a critical mass for change. SVP differs from more traditional planning approaches because SVP is "front-loaded." If the committee is successful in recruiting the steering committee and welcoming stakeholders to community conversations and task forces early in the process ("up front"), the planning process will be well on its way to success.

11. Listening Leaders Match People to Volunteer Opportunities

All of our congregations say they want to recruit more volunteers. Leaders who complete the Thriving Congregations Assessment strongly agree that their talents are known and that they feel personally welcomed and engaged. However, when they are asked about whether the congregation has a system to learn about the talents and interests of others and welcome their engagement, the scores drop sharply. In order to be a more effective leader, you need to first understand yourself. What makes you step forward? What makes you reluctant? Then you can better understand prospective volunteers.

Making the Match

A 2003 Urban Institute survey of volunteer management capacity among charities found that more than 40 percent of those who were no longer volunteering had withdrawn because of poor experiences they had had as volunteers (Urban Institute 2004). Not only has there been a decline in association, but those who have tried to "step forward" have often been disappointed. In the Urban Institute study, volunteers reported that their volunteer tasks were often poorly designed and were inadequately supervised or supported. People with little discretionary time often found that the volunteer work did not meet their expectations.

There are clearly barriers to volunteerism. What helps? One Jewish Federation did extensive interviews with prospective leaders between the ages of twenty-five and thirty-five. The following is a composite portrait I wrote about what I heard from these discussions:

Interviewer: Would you consider volunteering with the Federation?

Prospect: I don't really have the time.

Interviewer: Would you consider making time for this?

Prospect: I might if the work was really important.

Interviewer: What would it mean for the work to be important?

Prospect: I would want to know that this work would make a difference. I would also want to know that the work would be a good match for my talents.

Interviewer: What else would make you consider volunteering?

Prospect: I want to have staff support so that I can be confident that the project will be a success. On the other hand, I don't want the staff person to try to control everything. I'd want to have some autonomy.

My first instinct upon hearing this demanding wish list was to mutter (rather grumpily), "Is that *all* they want?" But if you use your active listening skills—and a little patience—you can better manage their conflicting desires, such as the need for both support and autonomy, or the desire to do important work while not spending a great deal of time on it.

Volunteer recruitment efforts face challenges today, and the next generation of potential volunteers (in their twenties and thirties) are even more discerning about what they will sign up for. Rabbi Joshua Rabin has written in his article "Will Your Synagogue Be a Club or a Cause?" that younger Jews are less focused on joining institutions and more focused on learning firsthand about their causes. They don't just want to join any organization; they look for projects they feel passionate about, with partners they want to work with. They judge by their own experience rather than by the norms of the past.

From our experience we have learned that prospective leaders want to use their talents; they want to make a difference; and they want to personally connect with the programs they develop. They value innovation, and they are less patient with slow bureaucratic responses. Tomorrow's volunteer development programs will need to look different. Designing and managing this volunteer outreach is strategic work.

12. Leaders Have the Courage to Hope

Most planning processes identify strengths and weaknesses. They look at the gap between the leaders' expectations and congregational performance. Most congregations, like most leaders, have certain strengths. Most congregations excel in certain areas (sermons, social action, education, leadership, etc.) or segments (young families, older adults, etc.). Part of the art of planning is to review the congregational landscape and to bring these various strengths into focus in order to inspire hope. Leaders should be able to make the case about what is great about their congregation and consider how they could build on this to better serve others.

The biblical spies who were sent to do reconnaissance of the Promised Land were encouraged to "take pains to bring back some of the fruit of the land" (Numbers 13:20). God knew that leaders needed to promise a sweet future in order to help sustain the people's hopes during their journey. SVP focuses on the positive. Our community conversations model begins with what is working and explores how we can build on those things. The Vision Builder Workshop starts with what we appreciate and asks how we can build on it. The task forces start out by creating a positive vision for their work. Congregations need to address problems, but they also need time to "pound their chest" about what is working well.

Pounding Our Chest with Pride

> It is not good for people to dwell too much on enumerating their sins, for it robs them of their joy and spiritual tranquility. Sometimes people should joyfully express the good they have done. (Rav Kook-Eyn Aya Maaser Sheni 5.10)

If you are reading this book or attending a workshop on this planning process, you are well aware of the challenges your synagogue faces and the shortcomings of your leadership. At our Yom Kippur service my rabbi invited us to reframe the High Holiday liturgy of the Ashamnu. Instead of beating our chest with guilt, he offered us a chance to celebrate some of the good things we have done in the last year. It can be a good thing to occasionally pound your chest with pride as you face a new year. Here is an adaptation of the list I created for leaders.

Hebrew	English	Doing Now	Could Do Even More
Ahavnu	We took time to love and appreciate our congregation.		
Berakhnu	We blessed our leaders. We put the spirit that we had upon them.		
Gamalnu Chesed	We acted with kindness under stress. We showed character.		
Darashnu	We searched creatively for solutions.		
Hiskalnu	We sought wisdom. We learned together.		
Yiganu	We worked hard. We were committed.		
Zacharnu	We remembered our synagogue at its best.		
Chizaknu	We grew stronger. We invested in leadership development.		
Kibadnu	We honored and recognized our leaders.		
Machalnu	We learned to forgive. We managed conflict constructively.		
Patachnu Yad	We opened our hands generously. We supported our synagogue.		
Kidashnu	We sanctified our work. We lifted up the sacred in our work.		
Tamakhnu	We supported each other.		
Tikkanu	We sought to repair our world, synagogue, and general community.		

Role Modeling the Change We Seek

We believe it is important to provide leaders a portrait of a strong and sacred leadership community. When we have examples of success, we need to call them out—we need to pound our chests. By lifting up a vision of effective leadership we can role model the changes we seek. The gates of our aspirational leadership community will open to such heartfelt efforts.

PART II

Understanding the Lay of the Land

Chapter 3
Foresight
Anticipating Synagogue Challenges

> *If people do not plow in the summer, what will they eat in the winter?*
>
> **—Midrash Mishle 6**

Synagogue leaders are responsible for looking to the future. As planners, they have been given the opportunity to look at their present situation and make some assumptions about the future. The most admired leadership skill, according to management scholars James Kouzes and Barry Posner (2002), is to provide an honest assessment of the environment. Our biblical ancestors had an agricultural tradition. They had to understand the changes in the seasons; they had to plan in order to survive. Synagogue leaders need to take time to understand and reflect on their environment and to invest in their communities' futures. God willing, they will be able to celebrate a bountiful harvest of new leaders, new projects, and new spirit (*ruach*).

1. Understanding the Synagogue Environment: Situation Analysis

Synagogue leaders often say to me, "It's just a shul. How complex can it be?" From a business perspective even small businesses can be complex to manage.

Leaders need to understand the forces they are managing. Only then can they productively debate the implications of these forces. In this book I am looking at trends in the United States as they impact liberal congregations. They have been the focus of my work. Other communities may find that many of these observations hold for them as well.

The Jewish world is changing fast. In Rabbi Sid Schwarz's *Jewish Megatrends*, we learn that many of the forces impacting synagogues (that is, intermarriage, having children later, distrust of institutions, costs of affiliation, growing diversity of members and their needs, etc.) are highly disruptive.

We ask leaders to be avid readers of the literature on synagogue leadership (for example, *Next Generation Judaism* by Mike Uram, *Sacred Strategies* by Isa Aron et al., *Jewish Megatrends* by Sid Schwarz, and *Relational Judaism* by Ron Wolfson). I am not trying to speak as an authority on trends but as a leader tasked with helping others manage their impact.

We ask leaders, "When you consider these trends and forces in your community, do you see them as having a high, medium, or low impact? Let's consider a few.

GI Generation and Next Gen

Many American synagogues were built in the 1950s and 1960s by the GI Generation. That generation put on a uniform and won a war. When they came home, many joined large corporations and organizations that stressed conformity. They built their suburban synagogues next to their Christian neighbors' churches. It was time of unusual convergence. They did not want to disrupt, they wanted to fit in.

The members of the GI Generation were joiners. They joined service clubs like the Rotary Club and Kiwanis, as well as trade associations and bowling leagues. Their kids went to schools that had only one approach to learning and where teachers were in charge.

We have come a long way from that world! My baby boomer generation wanted customization (our slogan: have it your way). Those under thirty expect to shape their own experience. One observer called it "playlist Judaism," referring to the way people create their own downloaded music libraries and arrange their songs in a playlist. While synagogues seek moments of convergence where they feel like one community, day to day they have to manage many diverse and often competing preferences.

Next Gen

Many young Jews are reluctant to join congregations. It is generational. When the Gallup Organization recently looked at American church membership, they found that 26 percent of all Americans reported that they have no religion. Of those who express some religion, many choose not to affiliate or worship in a congregation. Forty-two percent of millennials do not belong to a church. This trend of declining affiliation has really accelerated in the past twenty years (Steve Jones 2019).

Many of the same forces that are changing church affiliation patterns are impacting Jewish congregations as well. Synagogues are going to need to make a compelling case about why the next generation needs to belong in order to meet their communal and spiritual needs. They don't feel compelled just to join.

We have all heard the cry, "What are we going to do about next gen?" Many Jews today experience little Jewish learning or meaningful community from the time they have their bar or bat mitzvah until they are married. Young Jews are marrying later and having children later. The old synagogue membership model that depended on a steady flow of families putting their kids through the school has been impacted by these demographic changes. Synagogue membership efforts reach out to next gen, but they find a population that has spent a long time unaffiliated.

While there is a wide range of resources available today to engage young Jews, such as teen programs, camps, and Israel experiences, many young Jews still fall through the cracks in their teens and twenties. It is certainly the job of Jewish community leaders to build up these resources and ensure a better process for making the connections between one phase of Jewish life and another. While many synagogues will not be able to build this network on their own, they can do their part to contribute to this effort.

> In order to thrive, congregations need to find new partners, resources, practices, and sources of support. They need to think and act strategically.

See Change Coming: The Den Collective

A group of Conservative rabbis in the suburbs of Washington, DC, realized that they had to do something to meet young Jews *where they are* and help them connect with a rabbi, with each other, and with an authentic and meaningful Judaism, in their own neighborhoods. Rather than wait for these young people to find one of their synagogues, these leaders collaborated and made the following realization: *It was a tough realization for our synagogue partners that many of us had tried and failed to engage this demographic in a sustainable and fulfilling way. Geography, lack of critical mass, and a sense that current synagogue culture was not a great match for this group seemed like insurmountable challenges to overcome. As rabbis and congregations, we know we have a Judaism that is dynamic, passionate, and capable of creating powerful Jewish experiences. But how do we change ourselves to engage this next generation?*

[Mike] Uram argues that what he calls "disruptive" change is inevitable—the only question is whether organizations can see it coming (think about what happened to Kodak when photography moved to your smartphone) and adapt. But existing customers value current products and resist new initiatives. (Blumenthal and Schwartzer 2018)

These rabbis understood that strategic leaders need to see change coming. While congregations need to work with others (like the Millennials Project) to strengthen the network, each congregation should be accountable to make themselves more welcoming and better at integrating new members of all kinds. They *can* make their communities more open to the next generation. They *can* create outreach efforts to meet people where they are. SVP helps synagogues think about these issues and helps them strengthen their communities so that they will be around to welcome the next generation when they are ready.

Intermarriage and Inclusion

Synagogues were ethnic enclaves in the 1940s and 1950s. Anti-Semitism was a real concern. Jews were not fully accepted in many sectors of American life. Jews needed synagogues as community centers. Today Jews are welcome in most professions, families, and parts of American life. With growing acceptance, there has been growing intermarriage of Jews and non-Jews.

In the 1970s the percentage of couples that intermarried was about 17. Today it is well over 50 percent. In some parts of the country intermarriage is close to 70 percent.

In the Conservative Movement, rabbis are not permitted to marry interfaith couples. Nevertheless, being unable to officiate at the wedding does not mean that the synagogue does not include both members of the couple in the life of the congregation. Conservative synagogues are expanding the ways in which they include non-Jewish partners in Jewish learning, ritual, and lifecycle events.

Most young couples who are intermarried have close friends in interfaith families. They expect their fellow congregants to be welcoming and inclusive to interfaith families.

This is part of a larger and growing trend challenging synagogues to be more inclusive of LGBTQ households, people with disabilities, people of color, etc.

COVID-19 Crisis

During the coronavirus pandemic, congregations are learning to think beyond their walls. They are using virtual programs to welcome less engaged members and prospects. Leaders have learned to collaborate with other congregations and communal organizations to develop plans for opening their synagogues and schools. These adaptations and many others have increased their capacity for innovation. Will leaders be able to build on the foundational leadership skills of collaboration and innovation post crisis?

COVID-19 is creating many financial stresses, but it is also creating opportunities for innovation. As I note in my article "Emerging Leadership Lessons from the Crisis" (Leventhal 2020), whether a trend seems good or bad, it must be managed.

Question

As you consider these trends and forces in your community, do you see them as having a high, medium, or low impact?

2. Understanding the Synagogue as an Organization

Synagogues present challenges to leaders trying to create cohesive communities in a world of change. According to Susan Shevitz (1995), synagogues are distinguished by five characteristics: they are voluntary, pluralistic, loosely coupled, nonrational, and technologically weak. The following are my reflections on these characteristics.

Voluntary

Volunteers go in and out of the organization. They are interested in some issues and not others. They may have a period of high energy and then fade when other competing interests capture their attention. Authority in a voluntary environment is diffuse, writes Jim Collins (2005). There is not enough concentrated authority to ensure executive leadership. Leaders cannot coerce volunteers or pay adequate incentives for performance. This also means that accountability is weak, if present at all.

Pluralistic

Congregations today, as we mentioned earlier, have a diverse membership with diverse needs. As we noted, we are far from the convergence of the GI Generation. Unlike some businesses that can specialize (Just Jeans), most congregations have to serve a broad constituency. They are not able to fully segment their programs and focus on just a few profitable niches. They have a blueprint for community that comes from Torah, not from a business plan. Congregational leaders often must find a way to hear the voices of families with preschool children as well as empty nesters. They also need to anticipate the needs of singles and seniors. They need to manage the expectations of prospective members, new members, and longstanding members.

Loosely Coupled

Congregants may connect to some individuals and not to others. They may identify with some elements of the congregation's mission and not others. Synagogue observers have noted that many members have a "consumer orientation" rather than a membership orientation. The consumer is "loosely coupled." They may like a certain program or may enjoy some social events. They may be focused on getting their child a bar or bat mitzvah. They may not see the holistic mission of the congregation and all of the diverse voices that make up the community.

Limited Number of Core Leaders

In reviewing Shevitz's organizational characteristics, I have decided to add one feature I see often: the dedicated core leadership. Sales's study of Westchester congregations (2004) found that 5 percent were greatly active and another 14 percent were very active. This study thus found a core group of 19 percent. Most groups concur with this assessment. These are the people you can count on to see at services at least twice a month. They come to major events. They are working with some committee or group each year.

One of the challenges of synagogue life is to help the inner circle find ways for the less engaged to connect and be more active. That is why I ask leaders in chapter 1 to talk about one thing that they feel is thriving and how they could build on it to engage others. We need core leaders to be more generative.

It is not uncommon for the very active to spend years overfunctioning to keep the synagogue running. As they do this, they often become set in their ways. They develop a style of doing business. When new ideas are presented, they may say, "That won't work. We've tried that before." Some dominant leaders may interrupt a conversation and redirect the discussion to their approach. Intentionally or unconsciously, core leaders can resist innovation.

Developing leaders entails not only the challenge of recruiting and orienting new leaders but also ensuring that there are real leadership opportunities available for them. This means term limits for current members and structuring board meetings so that they elicit new ideas. It means that good procedures and practices (*derekh 'erets*) should be maintained to protect new ideas and new leaders.

Honoring Our Traditions

I was conducting a visioning workshop with a large historic multigenerational congregation. The older, more longstanding members were frustrated. They felt there had been too many changes in the congregation. At first they complained that new members were trying to "water down" Conservative Judaism. This charge tended to create conflict because it devalued the ideas of some newer members. As the process developed the older members became more explicit about their concerns.

They were upset that their tunes had been changed by the new cantor. Others were concerned that their High Holiday seats had been changed. Some were uncomfortable with some of the new approaches of the board. When they were asked to express all of these feelings as values, they argued that the congregation should "honor the synagogue's traditions." This was no longer a debate about who was a Conservative Jew. It was now developing into the issue of how to manage the rate of change and their fears of being marginalized.

I then asked them about the notes from the first workshop, when the planning group had decided that the synagogue needed to attract new members. The older members had all agreed this was a top priority. I asked if new members would want to come into a culture and agree not to change anything. The older members all laughed. They saw the absurdity of trying to hold on so tightly. In fact, all the stakeholders saw the irony of this. They realized that they would have to find ways to honor longstanding members while respecting the perspectives of new members if they were to achieve their membership goals.

Nonrational

Scholars note that in business organizations there is a great deal of irrationality. Managers bring complex emotions to their work. Today business leaders speak of organizations as "swamps," where the footing is unstable and the visibility blocked, metaphorically speaking, by "heavy foliage and mist." If businesses are sometimes swampy, what are congregational environments like?

In business organizations, at least people are in the same industry. Many share similar professional training. In contrast, synagogue leaders come from different industries, with a wide array of talents, experiences, and beliefs. Volunteers come with strong attachments, memories, beliefs, and positions. Many of these feelings lie below the surface and are not known at first to their congregational teammates. These emotions can come forward unexpectedly and without warning.

The Unexpected Agenda Item

Synagogue leaders have talked about the dread they have about certain issues. They recall how at their dinner table at home they shared their anxiety with their spouse. "Issue three is on the agenda tonight. It is going to be hot. We have heard the buzz about this for months, and now it's coming to the board. I will be late tonight, dear." When they get to the meeting, issue three sails through with only modest discussion. It turns out that issue four, the religious school field trip, is the hot one. How can this be? Why are experienced board members often so wrong about which issues will be controversial?

Unbeknownst to the board members, issue four is an important personal issue to a few congregational members. They remember the poorly planned school field trip from three years ago. Their children were on the bus that came late and did not have enough box lunches. It is an emotional issue for them. They forget about lay staff boundaries. They do not give the rabbi time to consult with the educator, even though she has the logistical details that might put their concerns to rest. They want to hash these out in the middle of the meeting of the entire board. They forget the board's agenda and its priorities, even though other issues clearly are of greater weight to the vast majority of the room. Issue four "turns out to be hot." Who would have guessed?

SVP CASE

Weak Information Technology

Most congregations keep poor records of the work product of committees and task forces. Therefore leaders are not able to share accurate information on membership trends, financial giving, or volunteer involvement. They are not able to discuss and debate written goals. Lack of key information in these areas can lead to poor decisions.

File on a Holiday

When I do SVP, I have several precontracting discussions about the process. One task is to identify the kind of data the planners need and determine what is available. As I begin to go down my checklist, the other party often goes silent. I have to check to see if the person is still on the line. I sense some anxiety about the depth and accessibility of the congregation's data.

In one instance I tried to offer a simple confidence-building request. I asked, "Can I get a copy of the minutes of the education committee?" My planning partner answered, "I will check, but I think she went to Boca." Went to Boca? I wondered. How can the education committee's records have gone to Boca?

The answer is that, like in so many congregations, there are few central files for the committees. They are the special preserve of individuals. The process is highly informal. Some take good minutes. Some hold on to them. Few ensure they are maintained or transferred to new leadership groups.

Historically Jewish learning was extremely serious about preserving the legal debates between scholars. We read about this rabbi's and that rabbi's views. Even the minority views that did not prevail were maintained. Despite this deep historic concern for honoring the past work of others, most synagogue leaders have very inconsistent and sketchy records. What few are available may have headed south to Boca.

3. The Synagogue's Context

All synagogue leadership approaches are affected by the synagogue's context and culture. In SVP, the context is the congregation's history, environment, and culture. It is made up of the stories that members tell. Context consists of the memories that members have and the meaning they make from memorial plaques and other artifacts that they encounter. Context is the size of the congregation as well as its history of size changes. Context is the way the governance functions and where decisions are processed. Context is the way that the rabbi has chosen or not chosen to lead. It is the authority the congregation gives to the rabbi, to Torah, and to halakhah. Context is the informal set of customs and practices that members observe when they do their synagogue work. Leaders must be aware of the congregation's size, culture, and lifecycle stage as elements of its context.

Congregational Culture

Rabbi Sam Joseph of Hebrew Union College once told me that every congregation has a DNA, an underlying character and culture. Congregations may change, but there are usually limits to their flexibility. There will be strong internal pressure to pull them back to where they were. Leadership should use the process of reflection to become more aware of their underlying culture. They will find it helpful to reflect on how they "do synagogue."

Communal scholars talk about a kind of congregation that is "all encompassing." When you join, you enter a community. You embrace its vision and goals. You become a "Member by Choice." Many congregations have a very diverse membership. Some join for convenience. Some join because their friends or family are there. Some join for a program, such as a good religious school. Given the nature of synagogue organizations, most congregations, according to Isa Aron, are not likely to be all encompassing communities with "Members by Choice": "All-encompassing congregations tend to be very traditional, very new or very small. It is nearly impossible to rewind the clock and turn large and/or heterogeneous synagogues back into communities of choice" (2002, 135). Any effort to "transform" synagogues must come up against these deep-seated cultural beliefs and practices.

Understanding your synagogue context and culture is an important step in planning.

Congregational Size

Arlin Rothauge has described four congregational size types (Gaede 2001, 15). I have translated this to households for synagogue use. They are family (up to 50), pastoral (50 to 150), program (150 to 350), and corporate (larger than 350). These are just general estimates. Many congregations operate with "one foot in several size cultures." As congregations change in size, they will make transitions into larger congregational structures or decline back to a previous size structure. While I am not going to try to explore all of these issues, you need to be aware that size affects the relationship of lay leaders to the professional staff, lay leaders to the clergy, and the clergy to the membership. For example, pastoral congregations require a great deal more hands-on managerial work by the lay leaders than a program congregation because there is inadequate staff to manage the work. Rabbis have more administrative responsibilities here and may describe themselves as "Jacks (or Jills) of all trades" in such congregations.

Congregational Lifecycle Stages

Congregations have various stages in their lives. Alice Mann, in *Can Our Church Live?* (1999, 2), describes congregational birth, formation, growth, stability, decline, and death. Different strategies and leadership styles are "appropriate" at each stage. Congregations "like biological organisms manifest a pattern of emergence and decline," which can be described with the following developmental arc.

1. Birth/The Dream: This stage reflects the earliest moments of a congregation's story. It may be the first meeting at someone's home or in a meeting room at the JCC. It may include the first Friday night Shabbat dinner when a service was put together.

2. Formation/Beliefs and Goals: During this phase the basic identity of the congregation takes form. For many congregations this starts with the family-size congregation, which is often lay led. At this stage the leaders are asking the following questions: Who are we? What are we here for? Who is our community?

3. Growth: The congregation has momentum. They have hired a rabbi and other staff. These are described as the "Glory Days."

4. Stability/Structure: The growth period paves the way for a period of sustainable congregational life. If the congregation has come through the formative stage and made the transition from family to pastoral and hired a rabbi, then years of stability may be supported on a firm foundation. This period includes the development of professional staff, operating procedures, facilities, financial resources, and governance processes. As time goes on, even stable congregations may come to a point of stagnation. When congregations are at the height of stability, it may be hard to motivate them to plan. These congregations are often quite satisfied with their situation. They lack the sense of urgency to work on long-term planning. They may prefer "problem-solving planning." Leaders sometimes need to disrupt this complacency.

5. Decline/Nostalgia, Questioning, and Polarization: At some point stagnation can turn into decline. As decline begins, writes Mann, "the congregation finds that it can no longer dismiss as temporary or random the noticeable falloff" (1999, 6). This falloff may be in members, worship attendance, lifecycle events, religious school enrollment, or High Holiday appeals.

I have seen many congregations moving from stagnation to periods of decline. As Mann notes, the most common response is to blame someone. When a community does not know what went wrong, they will often look for who went wrong. The rabbi may be blamed for a lack of vision, the lay leadership may be blamed for a lack of fundraising, or the congregation may be blamed for its apathy. As Mann observes, "The cycle of blaming tends to accelerate decline." One of the first things I try to do in such congregations is to shift the focus from blaming to looking at the entire congregational system to see how all of the elements contribute to the current situation and how leaders might contribute to the solution.

I try to shift the focus of leaders from fighting over tactical issues to exploring strategic ones. This is not easy because, as Mann writes of congregations in decline, "these congregations feel helpless about the changes in the external context so they are more likely to focus their attention on matters they feel they can control" (1999, 6).

In Alice Mann's model, during the decline stage, leaders have the option of restructuring their congregations or redeveloping them. When leaders restructure, they often try to work harder using the same people and the same tools. The alternative approach, redevelopment, calls for leaders to interrupt nostalgia in order to find new energy and direction. There may be some chaos and transition, but eventually a new dream may emerge and members can respond to that challenge.

4. Key Individuals Matter

I strongly believe in the systems approach to congregational analysis and leadership described here. I want to note, however, the important role played by key leaders of the congregation. Key leaders like Joshua can create bold new directions that part the waters of resistance. Poor leaders can plunge the congregation into chaos and conflict. Leadership is a function of the gifts of leaders (intelligence, awareness, self-management, etc.) and the challenges of their context (environment, leadership culture). The Jewish tradition appreciates the interplay of these factors. "According to one opinion, the character of a generation is determined by the leader. According to the other opinion the character of the leader is defined by the generation" (*b. Arakhin 17a*).

Look below the surface of a congregational conflict and you will see some powerful personality issues that dominate certain chapters of the story. Leaders are driven by a range of motivations. Some are inspired by our Torah tradition. Some seek control; some are trying to work through an issue with a member or staff person; some need status; some will stir things up to be in the limelight. Others are lonely and afraid to lose their place in the community. The motivating factors are many. Some are aware of their motivations, but for most they remain tacit and subconscious. Anyone who has worked with congregations in depth will attest to the impact that a few people can have on the direction of a congregation.

Conclusion

Many of the factors affecting synagogues are outside of the leadership's control. In a world of changes there are weaknesses to address and strengths to leverage. The synagogue organization is not a large business, but because of diverse membership and a special mission, it is complex. Leaders must learn to understand the synagogue context so that they can choose the right path (planning steps) to manage their congregation and ensure its future.

Questions for Reflection

1. If a reporter were doing a story on your congregation, how would they describe the environment or context around the congregation?
2. How would they describe the organization or culture inside the synagogue?
3. How does the surrounding environment and culture affect your leadership?

Chapter 4

Planning

Exploring Various Approaches

Go out and see which is the good way to which [one] should cleave.

—Avot 2:13

Joshua is charged with putting the people on the right path as they prepare to enter the Promised Land. He shows them where to cross the river. He commemorates their path by making a memorial of the stones they crossed on. Before they get too far on their journey, he reminds them of the covenant—the good path. Where can you find the good path for your congregation? I believe that the right path begins with the development of three plans: a leadership plan, a delegation/management plan, and an accountability plan.

The Leadership Plan

Given the challenges of the synagogue environment and the complexity of synagogue culture (chapter 3), it makes sense to invest in planning. Ronald Heifetz (1999) describes one of the benefits of planning as achieving the vantage point of "balcony space." High above the organizational stage a group of people can get out of "reactive space" and move on to the balcony to get the big picture and see how they fit into a much larger pattern. Congregations, as we noted, desperately need to get on the balcony space and away from reactive space. There they can look at their trends. On the balcony they become empowered to look at things in a new way.

In SVP planning leaders are joined by others "on the balcony" to see the big picture. In visioning work, this shared vantage point builds teamwork among planners. Chapter 3 discusses some of the data they might review from that vantage point.

The Leadership Plan

Alban has an instrument that evaluates congregations using systems theory, the Congregational Systems Inventory (CSI), developed by George Parsons and Speed Leas (1993). One of the seven dimensions that is analyzed is leadership. On one end of the continuum is the managerial pole, which is practical and tactical. On the other end is the leadership or transformational pole, which is visionary and strategic. Most congregational leadership groups are managerial and tactical. On a scale of one to ten, where one is managerial and ten is transformational, they will usually be between two and three.

According to Parsons and Leas, both styles of leadership are important. If you only think about mission and purpose, you might fail to balance the budget or pay the utility bill. If you are only focused on the utility bills, you may not pay enough attention to why you are maintaining the building. In Jewish terms, you need to balance the tension between 'erets (practical, earthly) and shamayim (spiritual, visionary). As the psalmist says, "Without a vision the people perish." Management and leadership are polarities; they are not problems to be solved but tensions to be managed. If leadership goes too far to one pole, it is harder to stay in touch with the imperatives of the other pole. When you get too far on the managerial pole, you simply forget what it's like to dream. You forget to ask why. When someone comes with an idea from the visionary realm, you may not recognize the gift they bring. Leaders are not consciously trying to be reluctant; they are sometimes simply unable to hear the message from the other pole.

Managers will not move to the leadership pole without a nudge. I hear synagogue leaders say, "We have important financial issues to review. Our meetings are too long already. We don't have time for this planning stuff." They don't feel they have time to invest in preparing for the future.

For years I gave this Parsons and Leas assessment to presidents of Conservative Congregations at our Sulam for Presidents workshop. Over the years most groups were about a two on the scale. What happens if their leadership team does not have anyone more transformational? Who will help them explore developmental or structural change? Who will help them dream, to get out and visit the six or seven positions? Groups will look where the leader looks. They need some curious and open leaders.

One leader noted that board meetings always turned negative after the treasurer's report. Little dreaming occurred. Everyone focused on what couldn't be done. I suggested they move the treasurer's report later on the agenda. SVP helps by taking a group of leaders up to the "balcony space." From this vantage point they can explore big ideas and little changes like moving an agenda item.

We Built It and They Came

One congregation had gone through rapid growth from a small havurah of fifty to a congregation of five hundred members. Leaders saw the opportunity to grow and borrowed money to build a facility in this growth area. It worked! The congregation was full of young families. There were more than sixty b'nai mitzvah one year. Underneath this dynamic growth there were developing tensions. Leaders had many unanswered questions:

- Should we have grown so fast?
- Should we have become so child focused?
- Should we have taken on so much debt?

I thought it was time to "get up on the balcony" and look at the big picture. They had grown faster than their lay and staff processes could manage. Through planning and visioning exercises we strengthened their staff and leadership capacity. They laid a better foundation for financial giving from young families and the overall membership. They created a twelve-month fundraising calendar. They began to consider how to retain bar and bat mitzvah families through the teenage year and beyond. They didn't want to become just a transactional "bar mitvah mill." They started a family education program track on Sundays.

SVP CASE

Delegation/Management Plan

Any kind of strategic or visioning work needs to connect the leadership plan with its question, "Where are we going?" to the delegation plan with its question, "Who will do what?" What are the specific roles and responsibilities and how can we set expectations of accountability when it comes to planning? In chapter 7 we will explore how SVP organizes the planning committee and in chapter 14 we will look at making assignments to task forces and defining the scope of these assignments. A well-defined delegation plan defines the tasks and empowers the team to work on the issues over a defined timeframe.

Accountability Plan

The planning process will only be effective if there is an emerging culture of accountability. The planners need to develop strategies, goals, and actions for all of their recommendations and communicate them to the board and planning leaders. In this way they develop accountability to themselves, their teams, and the congregation. If planning is successful, planning leaders will help demonstrate to the board the benefits of written strategies and goals and clear accountability.

Three Approaches to Planning

Alban consultants Gil Rendle and Alice Mann have described three kinds of planning in their book *Holy Conversations* (2003, 2).

1. Problem-Solving Planning

Problem-solving planning is for very specific concrete problems that can be solved with available knowledge. "Which bid on the paving should we take?" "Should we shorten the length of the congregational bulletin?" "What night should we have the book club?" These should be relatively short-term processes.

2. Developmental Planning

Many challenging congregational issues require developmental planning. The leadership needs to determine what the next stage is. There are now new congregational questions: "We have a new building. We have grown. What's next? How do we integrate the new members? Now that our larger membership provides us with more money, where should we allocate it?"

3. Frame-Bending Planning

Other congregations require frame-bending planning, which involves looking at the congregation's culture, its mission, its facility, and its neighborhood. Frame bending requires that leaders consider the shifts they need to make to address the changing situation. Shifts might be from depending on a few donors to creating a culture of giving or from having one approach to ritual to offering diverse options. These shifts stir the pot and may stir opposition.

There are often competing positions: those who want a one-day-per-week Hebrew school, and those who want to keep raising the bar of what can be taught; those who want more spirituality and innovation, and those who want the services to be exactly as they remember them growing up. Longstanding members talk about how things have always been, and newer members seem to show little reverence for the past.

These are not "problems to be solved." These are issues that require new learning and understanding. Leaders need to reflect on these diverse views before they can plan how these members can live more successfully and "Jewishly" together.

Most congregations require some measure of all three types of planning. There are always some who want to go directly to problem solving. When it comes to developmental and frame-bending issues, it doesn't pay to rush. The conversation needs to develop.

Technical Change versus Adaptive Change

Ronald Heifetz (1999) encourages planners to look at the roles of participants in the change process. He draws a distinction between technical change and adaptive change. Some changes can be done by experts. Some changes require that the people actively participate in the process of change. He calls these "adaptive changes."

Technical Change

Should we replace the air conditioning? Who should cut the grass? Should we increase the hours of the janitorial staff? These issues are common committee tasks with technical solutions. The executive director, the house chair, or the service provider can usually describe the problem, look at alternative solutions, and make a decision without much input from the system.

In a technical change, a few people can be responsible for all of the knowledge and skills. Consider the work of a surgeon. In terms of the operating procedure, the level of participation by the patient is usually relatively low, and the concentration of power in the expert specialist is relatively high.

Adaptive Change

Adaptive change is more like a therapeutic relationship. The patient must make an effort to share important information and insights with the therapist. Most liberal congregations (non-Orthodox) must wrestle with how much they should change to mirror the trends, forces, and factors of their contemporary culture. Amy Asin of the Union for Reform Judaism calls this sensitivity the organization's "porousness." Judaism has many values that are countercultural. Living in the tension between tradition and modernity takes a communal conversation. In a congregational setting, this means that a wide array of congregational stakeholders must agree to learn from the planning process and to practice the new skills they have acquired.

Conclusion

In order to plan, you need to know if you are primarily trying to problem solve, do developmental planning, or do frame-bending planning. Frame-bending planning requires adaptive change. All plans have some of each approach, but there is usually an overarching approach that defines the scope of the work. The more adaptive the process of change, the more time it will require and the more people it will need to be engaged in the learning.

Questions for Reflection

1. What are your technical problems to solve?
2. Where do you need developmental change?
3. Where do you need more adaptive structural change?

Chapter 5
Congregational Readiness for Change

Before God confers office on a man, he first tests him with a little thing and only then promotes him to greatness.

—Shemot Rabbah 2:3

This text refers to the way God tested Moses. God first observed how Moses cared for his sheep in the wilderness. Then God trusted him to shepherd a nation. You need to make an honest assessment of your leadership. You need to see how they are doing the basics, the little things, before you ask them to embark on shepherding the congregation through SVP, a very challenging thing. Have they been launching task forces? Have they been wrestling with tough issues? Have they been practicing collaboration? These efforts can show readiness to do a big new thing.

While I am very enthusiastic about SVP's various tools and processes, many of the leadership groups I see have low energy for this type of work—like the spies, they are reluctant. Many have long memories of failed projects and unresponsive members. They can tell you about the event they planned for one hundred that drew only forty. It broke their hearts.

As planners we often hear the refrain, "We tried that already." While this can be frustrating, we should not gloss over the planners' underlying concerns. They provide invaluable information about past hurts, disappointments, and frustrations. These experiences were real for them, and we will not be able to move forward successfully by ignoring them.

Evaluating Congregational Readiness

Before I agree to work with a planning team, I determine if the leadership is ready for the task. Congregations are different. Some are doing well and there is no urgency to do developmental planning now. Others lack a readiness to plan. I have developed some characteristics of successful planning teams for leaders to consider. If a congregation does not have enough of these assets, they may need to set more modest planning goals. They may not, however, be a candidate for serious twelve-month planning.

All congregations have informal norms that they don't articulate. They have deep unconscious (tacit) norms that they may not even be aware of. The planning team must be humble about the ability of new plans to overcome the underlying DNA of the congregation. Planners need to check for readiness to plan but also expect the inevitable surprises along the way. Let's look at some of the things that can affect readiness and focus.

SVP Readiness Factors

1. The Rabbi Must Be Supportive, Enthusiastic, and Committed to Planning

While the staff and lay leadership play key roles, if the rabbi is not committed to the planning process, it will be hard to sustain change. Programmatic initiatives that require professional staff to follow up may lose focus. When the rabbi is not ready, it does not make sense to embark on visioning and planning. Lay leaders can certainly use the tools in this book for lay leadership development or transition planning, but the multiyear commitment required for planning and implementation is too great without full rabbinic support.

Sometimes a congregation will explore planning to help them prepare to welcome a new rabbi, but I don't recommend a full planning process without the rabbi on board and participating. We do not want to hand the new rabbi a "fully baked cake." We need their input and their vision. Doing a survey or a few focus groups on behalf of a search committee, however, might be an appropriate scope of work in this situation.

2. Commitment of the Board President to Planning Efforts

SVP is at least a twelve-month process, and the ideas and initiatives that come forward in planning need to be implemented over a twelve- to twenty-four-month period—or longer. This means the board president, both current and incoming, needs to be involved and committed. We can look at biblical history and find moments of successful transition such as Moses to Joshua and periods of instability when there was little intentional succession planning—see the book of Judges. When succession is not planned, much of what the prior leadership has learned is lost.

3. There Must Be Urgency for Change

Some congregations are performing quite well. They may be in a great location with wonderful demographics for new members. They may have experienced and effective professional and lay leadership. These congregations may feel that their current governance and the leadership and management tools they have are adequate. They may not feel the need to mobilize a planning committee and stakeholders to do SVP. They may simply want a small committee or task force to upgrade financial plans. If the urgency is not there, it will be very difficult to launch the process, and even harder to keep it going.

4. Key Lay Leaders Must Be Committed to Planning

Even with the involvement of the board president, the rest of the board must also be committed and engaged in the process. In each stage of planning, there will be opportunities where the board will be asked to participate (for example, community conversations and vision builder sessions) or join a team (for example, the steering committee and task forces). They will also be expected to take part in the data-gathering process. And of course it is the board that is ultimately responsible for approving the plan, and so it would be completely irresponsible of them not to ask questions and to participate and engage when asked by the planning team.

   With all that said, when I get a request to come in, the leaders are seldom in complete agreement about doing planning. Some might decide not to endorse the final plan. Others may actively oppose the process.

Still others might be passive aggressive. They may listen but not agree to participate when asked or take part in implementation. When starting the planning process, I try to review the steps of the plan with the core leadership, board, and senior staff. This models the kind of consensus-building skills needed later in the process.

5. There Needs to Be Some Financial Commitment to Planning

Planning requires resources. Even if a congregation uses this book to self-guide their process, they will need to budget for meals, the preparation of materials, etc. Most congregations will want to bring in some kind of outside facilitator to do the Vision Builder and Priority Setting workshops. This requires a planning budget. The process of getting some money in the next year's budget for planning will bring all of the other readiness issues into better focus. When the board has to vote on spending the money, they will dig deeper to explore their readiness. That is a very good thing.

> If the congregations are not investing any of their own funds, they may not be as invested in the planning.

6. Planning Should Not Be Directly Competing with Other Major Projects

Congregations during SVP need to be focused. They cannot be distracted by another major congregation-wide project. If they are in the midst of doing a capital campaign or at the start of a building campaign, they may not be ready for SVP. There is seldom enough energy to do both tasks. I once worked with a congregation in which a capital campaign was going on just before SVP began. The congregation had just gone through parlor meetings, interviews, and presentations as part of the capital campaign. They were drained.

In this kind of situation, I would suggest a short-term leadership development training rather than a whole congregation visioning plan.

7. Planning Requires Some Capacity for Creativity

Some congregations have little capacity for creative vision exercises. They are so resistant to change that they won't allow stakeholders room to brainstorm. They tend to interrupt brainstorming verbally or nonverbally. They discourage creative thinking in group sessions.

Older established leaders remind new leaders that their ideas "have been tried before." They provide background information on why the culture won't respond to a proposed idea. They provide institutional memory, most of it negative. We need leaders who will bring the best of their past to the service of their future—not their past failures. I designed SVP to keep workshops fun, fast paced, engaging, and future focused. I put a premium on creativity and collaborative learning to help overcome the reluctance of some stakeholders and the negativity of the past.

8. Planning Requires a Tolerance for Feedback

Some congregations are not used to getting feedback. They don't have much of a history of trust. It follows that these groups are often reluctant to empower new individuals or groups. Empowered groups will provide the leadership with the opportunity for new energy and creativity (as I noted earlier), but they will also provide some challenging feedback. They will ask questions and raise concerns. Knowing that feedback raises anxiety, I make a special effort to focus on the strengths of the congregation and explore opportunities to build on these.

9. Full SVP May Not Be for Congregations Facing Major and Irreversible Demographic Decline

Some geographic locations are facing overwhelming demographic changes. The community may be aging; there may be few students for school; housing costs may have soared; and the congregation's neighborhoods may no longer be affordable for young families. Some areas have a changing socioeconomic mix; crime may be a factor; and the old neighborhood may not seem safe. If the community is facing overwhelming demographic decline, they may lack the energy and hopefulness to recruit a large stakeholder group.

One of the features of leadership groups who have experienced years of decline is that they lose the capacity to attract new leaders, new ideas,

In redevelopment you don't focus on expanding all of the missions you are dreaming up. You focus the congregation's limited resources on a few missions you have capacity for.

and new energies. In these cases we have to work with the limited energy we can find. Congregational redevelopment, as we mentioned, uses some SVP tools but in a more limited and focused way (see Mann 1999).

10. Planners Must Be Able to Manage Conflict

Potential SVP congregations should not be in the midst of a high-level conflict. It is too difficult to recruit participants when people are in warring camps. SVP requires a lot of energy. You have to sell others on the value of planning and its value to the congregation. Planning is somewhat abstract. Congregations need to trust in the assumptions and processes of SVP. In a culture where trust is strained and conflicts are raging, it is hard to get people to trust you.

Some congregations fail to fully describe this history of conflict in the pre-planning phase. It lies, like an iceberg, below the surface. Some leaders simply don't understand the full scope of what happened. Others may be driven to portray themselves, through revisionist history, in a more favorable light. If you have a major conflict, it is important to delay SVP and work to acknowledge the conflicts and mediate the concerns of the various parties. If you don't delay, the conflict may emerge in the middle of the planning process.

Conclusion: Taking the Right Journey

Are you ready to do planning? While not every congregation is ready for a full planning process, most boards can benefit from a board retreat that helps clarify vision, values, strategies and goals.

Questions for Reflection

1. How ready is your congregation for visioning and planning?
2. How ready is your congregation for leadership development?
3. What would increase your team's readiness to plan?

Chapter 6
Managing the Campaign

It is not your duty to complete the work but neither are you free to desist from it.

—Avot 2:16

Planning leaders need to understand how they and their teams are going to manage the process of change. They need to find ways to communicate what they are learning about the planning journey. Each individual and each team will experience change differently, but our hope is that if you work with this book, you will have the tools you need to successfully embark on this sacred journey. This book is about fostering strategic thinking. We do not feel every president needs to complete a plan, but every president needs to make a start toward more strategic leadership.

Why Do Congregational Leaders Resist Change?

Congregational consultants talk about a system in homeostasis. There is a "comfort zone" that the culture has established. Why do leaders fail to get started with plans? Many congregations get stuck in that comfort zone. They often don't recognize that they are stuck. Most congregational leaders are managerial. They are not the leaders who go up to the balcony space to look at the long-range picture and begin to ask challenging questions.

Dr. Gil Rendle notes that "leaders who set things in motion make it hard for managers of the status quo to maintain stability" (1999, 64). Those managers may not appreciate their limitations being brought to their attention. One of the challenges of leadership is to encourage new perspectives, even if they create some uneasiness. Change leaders can become lightning rods for what Rendle calls "free-floating anxiety" (33). They can find themselves out on a limb, where they are very vulnerable.

All too often synagogue presidents become the focus of resistance. Too often they don't get a large enough group of people to support their initiatives. In the face of this resistance, some presidents may try to work even harder to make things happen and end up burning out. Those who face too much change alone may make a sudden exit after their presidential terms and take with them valuable insights and experiences. Our biblical narrative shows how Joshua intentionally creates a procession of priests, leaders, and others when he crosses the Jordan, and they begin their next chapter together on the other side.

> SVP was designed to create a large group of planners so that a few change leaders would not become the lightning rods of resistance to change.

A Sense of Fear and Loss with Change

When you empower and energize new people, new ideas and approaches come to center stage. Existing leaders may not welcome all of these new "co-creators." They will not have the usual control of the discussion. They may not be able to use Robert's rules to call others out of order. New ideas are popping up on flip charts all around the room. Existing leaders may feel out of their comfort zone and feel that they are being pushed off the stage. They may have memories of a "golden age" of the congregation.

To engage in effective planning, experienced leaders need to be willing to accept new processes, ideas, and initiatives. At this same time, new leaders need to have compassion and understanding for those who came before them and dedicated their lives to the synagogue community.

In our biblical story, some challenged God's plan and rejected the idea of entering the land. One commentator noted that the names of the spies suggested that many were shepherds. When these shepherds heard that the land would be flowing with milk and honey and when they saw the sample of giant grapes so large they had to be carried by two men, instead of joy, they saw loss—loss of wealth, loss of power, loss of prestige. They were ungrateful for God's redemption if it meant the future was in farming. Look around your congregation. If you begin to make changes, who might feel a sense of loss?

The community went through a lot of chaos before it regrouped to cross the Jordan into the land of Canaan. In the biblical narrative most of the people ultimately decided to stop complaining and follow Joshua.

Energetic, Tenacious Leadership

In order to undertake a visioning and planning process, leaders must maintain an above average level of energy. That is why, when we consult, we probe in order to explore a congregation's readiness to plan with us (chapter 5). We want to establish whether they are able to face resistance and overcome it.

We see this tenacity in Moses. Even after he was punished for striking the rock (Numbers 20:12), he pulled himself together and went back to his leadership responsibilities. Even after God told him that he would not go into the land, Moses took up his responsibilities as a leader. He got right back to work and began negotiating passage for his people with the king of Edom (Numbers 20:14–17).

Creating and Sustaining Change

Peter Senge (1990) has described organizations as having reinforcing loops and balancing loops. In a reinforcing loop, projects gain momentum. They gain allies and resources, and people talk about how things are "really flowing." In a balancing loop, projects slow down and people talk about how they are "stuck."

SVP tends to work on strengthening the reinforcing loops that lead to new practices and create momentum. As primarily volunteer organizations, synagogues are somewhat inefficient operations. The best projects can get bogged down in the congregational swamp. Given these patterns of resistance (balancing loops), sustained change processes are quite difficult and uncommon. Leaders need to keep up momentum even when change is difficult to manage, or they will get stuck. Sharing a short-term win that comes out of the planning process can help demonstrate that change is possible.

I have noted that change can move forward in one area and slip back in another. Even the most promising planning work can be derailed by a change in presidents, a change in the professional staff, some external factor, or a conflict with the rabbi. For this reason, most planning teams need to be flexible in the specifics of their work while staying true to their mission, purpose, and strategies.

SVP: The Campaign of Change

SVP understands that planners can go through difficult stages. Each step is important, and leaders must maintain momentum through the process. Harvard professor and management consultant John Kotter argues that planning leaders must address key change management elements in order to maintain momentum for change (1999). I have adapted them here.

1. Establish a Sense of Urgency

SVP clarifies the critical issues that need to be addressed in the data-gathering phase. When you agree to hold community conversations and gather data, you are confirming that you want to identify key issues. You are moving away from an attitude of denial to a place of openness and curiosity.

Leaders must explain that the work of planning requires above average effort. It takes energy to overcome the tendency toward avoidance and denial. One of the greatest barriers to change is the limited amount of energy available for planning. One congregational leader asked me, "How can you argue for such an intense process while acknowledging that volunteerism is in decline?" I agree: it is an apparent contradiction.

> Most turnarounds require that the leaders make a major investment in energy to take the organization to the next level.

It is not realistic to expect that the average leadership team will always sustain a high level of effort, but in order to build an infrastructure of data, values, and goals, it requires a significant up-front investment of time. The teams must agree to work at a higher level for a while. If you have not established a "sense of urgency" at the start, you will have a very difficult time getting the level of support and engagement that is needed for a successful planning effort.

2. Form a Powerful Guiding Coalition

In SVP we insist on meeting with the rabbi, the executive committee, and the senior staff to get their input. We also recruit and train the steering committee. When a steering committee of eight to twelve people has been put together to lead the process, and an additional twenty-five to sixty people have been recruited for task forces, a powerful guiding coalition will have been created. These stakeholders represent different segments of the community, so they create a "buzz" of energy.

This is not the average planning group. It has a symbolic power when it emerges from the congregational scene. Others in the community sense that "something is happening." Traditional gatekeepers who have been able to avoid certain conversations (the balancing loops) see that this powerful guiding coalition is less likely to be sidelined.

3. Create a Shared Vision of the Future

SVP requires a Vision Builder workshop after the data is gathered. This helps to create a shared language for the work throughout the process. Many people ask me why we don't start the process by working on a new mission and vision statement. I do give the steering committee, as part of the initial training, a worksheet to analyze their current mission statement if they have one. Most leadership groups do not have enough shared knowledge about the congregational environment, however, to write a mission statement or charter task forces at the start. They need to come together as a team first and then build a vision together later.

4. Communicate the Hopeful Vision

SVP encourages creating scenarios of the future. You will share what you've learned about environmental trends and members' wants and needs with the congregation. Opponents of planning often focus on the negative. I try to instill in leaders the principle that while there are many elements of the synagogue they cannot control, they can control their attitudes. Few people want to volunteer for a negative leadership. Attitude matters! The SVP process creates an opportunity. Successful planners seize the day and unleash new positive energy.

5. Empower Others to Act on the Vision

SVP convenes a visioning session for the board, staff, and steering committee called the Vision Builder workshop. A diverse group of voices is heard. Small group discussions put an emphasis on participation. These sessions communicate that "all ideas matter." People are challenged to resist being judgmental. Many boards are dominated by a few strong personalities. When the facilitator uses the visioning process to break down these organizational walls, a lot of new energy flows.

We empower leaders to create a vision for each of the critical focus areas they want to pursue. They are then asked to make a list of tasks that the task force should address to put the vision into action. They will hand this work off to the task force once it is formed. As the process evolves we invite people to join four to seven task forces. We will invite the congregation to community meetings to hear about emerging task force ideas. In all these ways we are inviting others to act.

6. Plan Short-Term Wins

SVP creates a "wish list" from all committees and staff so that planners are aware of volunteer opportunities. One of the central needs identified by most congregations is for better volunteer management. SVP shows planners the potential talents and gifts of members. It elicits ideas and projects. This outpouring of creativity encourages congregations to find a better way of identifying volunteer interests and monitoring how these are put to work in the congregation.

SVP hopes to create short-term wins that can create momentum for planning. Some teams create a fast-track process to assign ideas that come out of the community conversations to committees rather than wait for the creation of task forces. This is the "low-hanging fruit" that can be put into action immediately. Other larger initiatives that take more consideration, planning, and support should wait until the end of the planning process.

7. Consolidate Improvements

SVP creates a key initiative tracking process for the implementation stage to ensure follow up on strategies. SVP attempts to connect committees to the synagogue's mission, vision, and strategies.

Conclusion

Without a sense of urgency, leaders won't invest their energy in a change process. By developing a new vision together as one community, leaders will be able to paint a picture of the road ahead. Momentum in planning will be maintained when leaders of the planning process stay on track and can communicate their progress. Planning can cause alarm for those who fear change, but it can also bring new hope, life, and energy into the present and into the future.

Questions for Reflection

1. Have you seen planning projects lose momentum? What happened?
2. Think of a successful project that you participated in. What helped keep the team focused and energized?
3. What do you need to launch a campaign of change?

PART III

Getting Organized for the Journey

Chapter 7
Planning Committee Start Up

In our biblical story, Moses appoints leaders from the twelve tribes to go out and scout the Promised Land. They are like a strategic planning committee that is tasked to create a situation analysis. We hear little about their training. When they encounter adversity, they fall apart. They not only create an unbalanced report that focuses on the negative but they also lack the self-discipline to give their report to Moses. They don't go through channels. They panic and spread their anxiety throughout the camp.

Some planning processes create a leadership team but then immediately create subcommittees and task forces and send them out to do the work in separate areas. This siloes the strategic work of the various focus areas from the very beginning. In SVP we invest time in developing the leadership capacity of the planning team. We go slow and steady so that they can develop shared vocabulary and dream boldly together. We ask them to work for about six months before we launch task forces. We encourage the team to have a holistic understanding of the foundational issues.

Rabbi Steven Rein, of Agudas Achim Congregation in Alexandria, Virginia, participated in USCJ strategic planning:

"We are in the business of helping people find connections and experiences of wholeness through relationships." In fact, one of the benefits that Agudas Achim saw from the strategic planning process was that the planning committee bonded as a group.

We encourage leaders to build a planning team. We create a safe place for planners to do strategic work. By strengthening their team process, we hope they will not panic like the spies when they face adversity.

Rabbi and Professional Staff

If we are going to build team work, there should be a clear understanding about the staff's role. How can the staff help focus and support some of the new energy that will be created? SVP requires a partnership between the staff and the planning team. There are many opportunities for rabbis and other staff to bring their creativity to the process.

During the SVP process there is always pressure to cut the duration of the workshops. Planning challenges rabbis and other staff to reallocate their time. There are few substitutes for the power of effective clergy leadership in helping a congregation step forward. They are positioned to enrich the process and pastor to their leaders.

- Clergy can access the power of the traditional texts.
- Clergy are present in critical leadership meetings for staff and board members.
- Clergy can focus us on transcendent issues.
- Clergy can help current leaders remember how their ancestors were called to serve.
- Clergy can raise expectations for covenantal kindness (hesed).
- Clergy model the spiritual discipline leaders need.

Despite these opportunities, many clergy find it hard to convene the conversations they need to have with leadership. SVP provides the clergy with the chance to step forward and get important issues on the synagogue planning agenda.

Building a Planning Agenda

- Shared Understanding of the Planning Process: We review the change management process and share tips for how to handle resistance.
- Shared Assumptions about the Situation: We review internal and external data, including members' attitudes and needs. We review the results of their Thriving Congregations Assessment.
- Shared Mission and Vision: We ask the team to write an initial mission statement and create a vision statement for each focus area.

Text Study Reflection: The Birth of Rabbinic Judaism

The group explores the following text, which looks at a time when the Jewish people were at a crossroads and needed to manage change:

> When the holy day of Rosh Hashanah fell on Shabbat, in the Temple they would blow (the shofar), but not in the rest of the Land of Israel. After the Temple was destroyed, Rabbi Yochanan ben Zakkai enacted that they would blow in every place in which there is a Bet Din (court). Rabbi Eliezer said, Rabbi Yochanan ben Zakkai enacted only for Yavneh. They said to him, "It is the same whether in Yavneh or any other place in which there is a court." (Mishnah Rosh Hashanah)

In my article "The Change Management Plan," I discuss three types of change. We refer to these in chapter 4:

1. Problem-Solving Change: This is technical change in which we rely on experts to solve the problem.
2. Developmental Change: This is adaptive change in which people learn something together.
3. Structural Change: This is very adaptive change in which people join together and risk going through difficult transitions to build a new foundation for the future.

In this text, the rabbis needed to make a structural change. The Temple and its priests had been destroyed. They were not going to succeed by simply tweaking the liturgy. Rabbi Yochanan ben Zakkai and the leaders of the time needed to create a new, decentralized service where new rabbis would be welcomed and new practices would be developed. The shofar would need to be sounded to call the people in new places. Most congregations talk about innovation but often stay with the existing programs and priorities. This leads to a focus on small, problem-solving, short-term change. In this text they have to innovate by blowing the shofar in Yavneh and keep innovating to blow the shofar in new towns. The central place of worship is gone.

SVP CASE

Making Innovation a Priority

One of my Alban Institute colleagues worked with a congregation that wanted to reach out to a very diverse and changing community. Leaders constantly talked about the need for trying fresh approaches to engage members. He asked leaders to write down on a large sheet of newsprint all of their current programs. The participants filled up the paper with their programs. He then asked them to identify those that were addressing new members and less engaged members' needs. When the fact sheets were mounted where all could see them, it became very clear that few programs addressed those groups. The congregation clearly was not allocating resources commensurate with the importance they placed on doing new things.

Diagnosis, Dialogue, and Deliberation

In our planning process, we ask planners to review foundational data-gathering work so that they can deliberate about which task forces to launch. Planners begin by gathering data and diagnosing the problems to work on. Over time, they will engage in a variety of conversations so that they can tap the collective wisdom of the planners in these dialogues. As the process continues, more voices will be welcomed and new ideas will emerge. When we are dealing with technical change (the roof needs to be repaired), we can find someone who knows how to fix it, but when we are talking about adaptive questions such as reimagining Judaism after the destruction of the Temple or welcoming a next generation of young Jews, no one person usually has the answer.

> When we are talking about adaptive questions such as reimagining Judaism after the destruction of the Temple or welcoming a next generation of young Jews, no one person usually has the answer.

Leaders often lack the insight and energy to solve adaptive problems. The answers need to develop over time. Leaders today face many of these types of adaptive changes.

- How porous (open to changing culture) should the synagogue be to the trends and forces impacting the synagogue (see chapter 3)?

- Should we align with the culture or strive to be countercultural?
- How do we welcome the diversity of our members and still feel like one congregation?
- How do we develop the technical and political skills to launch critical experiments?

These are very adaptive questions. We need to help the team resist short-cuts and take the time to find the answers together. We ask planners to seek the recommendations of all their colleagues so that they can give adequate weight to all ideas.

Getting to Know Each Other and Building Trust

One of the key principles of planning leadership is that leaders should "role model the change they seek." If we want to engage our members, then we need to be an engaging planning team. If we want to understand our members' talents and interests, then we need to be curious about the strengths of our teammates and take the time to get to know them as individuals.

Leadership Profile

In order to make it easier to begin to get to know our teammates, we have created a leadership profile. In our opening exercise we ask the planning team to complete the profile and share one strength they hope to bring to their work on this team. We believe that this is a necessary step in building a foundation for the work of the team (see appendix resource 3). The chair collects these profiles to gain insight into their team.

Start Up Workshop Goals

- Clarify the planning process
- Help planning members get to know each other
- Explore different approaches to change
- Explain assignments to key teams of the planning committee

Prework

Read the first seven chapters of *Stepping Forward Together*.

Have board, staff, and planning committee take the Thriving Congregations Assessment (TCA).

Review results of the group's TCA together:

- Put a check mark next to major strengths.
- Put a question mark next to areas that need development.
- Use the TCA journal to write one strength to build on and one area that needs more development.

Annotated Guide: Planning Committee Start Up Workshop

Leader Profile: Ten Minutes

We ask all leaders to take the time to get to know each other by completing a short profile. The chairs can use this data to remind themselves of the interests and needs of team members. This helps leaders imagine how they might want to gather this information for others later. Invite each person to share the following:

- Name
- Number of years in the congregation
- One strength they hope to bring to planning

Norms to Guide the Team: Ten Minutes

We are trying to build a planning team. Members need to build trust so that they can feel comfortable sharing and accepting feedback over the course of the project.

We welcome participants to share some values that should shape our work. Some of these values might include:

- Openness: gather facts before rushing to assumptions
- Attendance: come to meetings, be on time
- Preparedness: prepare in order to contribute effectively to planning committee meetings and task force meetings
- Respect: listen to others, give them the benefit of the doubt

- Commitment: be willing to go the distance to finish the work, even if it is challenging
- Curiosity: be open to new people and new ideas

Text Study: Birth of Rabbinic Judaism: Ten Minutes
Review Process Steps: Fifteen Minutes
Review Three Teams: Fifteen Minutes
Questions: Fifteen Minutes

Data-Gathering Team

Some tasks include:

- Fact book: defines data that is available and works with staff to gather information
- Interviews of key committees
- TCA: give to planning committee and board
- Congregational survey: conduct congregational survey
- Create executive summary of survey: leads discussion with committee to analyze data and write emerging themes, leads data debrief session with board
- Present data at all task force meeting and town meetings
- Focus groups: explores the use of community conversations

Communications Team

Some tasks include:

- Create welcome note to planning team members
- Develop congregational letter announcing planning team and process
- Send invitation to members to participate in survey
- Work with president to provide communications in bulletin, sermons, addresses, etc.
- Write High Holiday message in bulletin
- Write profiles of planning team members (highlight in bulletin)
- Write stories of short term victories: low-hanging fruit
- Send invitation to all task force meeting
- Touch base with leaders, stakeholders, members

- Invitation for town hall meeting, congregation hears results, gives input
- Write final report

Mission and Vision Team

Some tasks include:

- Follow up on introductory mission reflection exercise done at start up meeting
- Review current mission statement, explore if it needs to be tweaked
- Conduct Vision Builder with steering committee and board
- Type up vision 1.0
- Edit and create vision 2.0
- Facilitate conversations at all task force meetings on mission and vision 3.0
- Create final overall congregational mission and vision statement
- Create shorter version, explore the creation of taglines, web copy (if desired)

Do Mission Refection Exercise: Fifteen Minutes

We ask leaders to complete TCA in advance. This creates some shared background. We then ask them to answer three questions about the mission of the congregation. The goal is not necessarily to write a new mission statement but rather to help build teamwork at the start up meeting. Our process is designed to help leaders reflect on their current environment and connect this insight to the synagogue's enduring mission.

The three mission questions are as follows:

1. What do we do? What is our desired outcome?
2. Who are we? Whom do we seek to serve (members, stakeholders, donors, supporters)?
3. What would we like to be known for (our niche, position, passion)?

Next Steps: Ten Minutes

- Mission team: write up notes from mission exercise, add some possible supporting actions
- Communications team: write congregational letter to introduce planning team to the congregation
- Data-gathering team: summarize TCA journals, do initial review of survey questions, review guide to community conversations, work on fact book
- Plan for second meeting: team reports, SWOT exercise (see chapter 11)

125 minutes

Chapter 8

Gathering Data

Understanding the Landscape

See what the land is . . . and whether the land is rich or poor.

—Numbers 13:18–20

Leaders need to know the lay of the land. Data gathering is a core element of planning. We need to know the congregation's past history and current situation before we dream about its future, but many congregations struggle to gather the critical data they need. What are some of the challenges we face as we approach the important task of gathering data?

The Challenges

Challenge #1: Leaders Don't Know Where to Get External Data

Many of the critical factors affecting the congregation are outside the control of its leaders. What is happening in your environment? What are the key demographic questions you should be asking? What are the trends? Congregational planners are usually not used to asking these questions, and they often don't know where to start.

Some good sources of external data include the following.

a. Jewish Federations. Local Jewish Federations have done Jewish population studies of many urban areas. When Federation studies are properly done and are current, they can be particularly helpful.

b. Pew Report. The Pew Research Center issued a report on Jewish Americans in 2013. It can be accessed here: https://www.pewforum.org/2013/10/01/jewish-american-beliefs-attitudes-culture-survey/. It provides many insights into the changing Jewish community. What is clear is that younger generations of Jews identify less as religious Jews and more as cultural Jews. According to this study, 32 percent of millennial Jews do not identify as Jewish by religion.

Other findings from the Pew study indicated that respondents believe in God, are proud to be Jewish, and have a sense of peoplehood around such issues as Holocaust remembrance. When it comes to a commitment to Jewish law and ritual, the identification was much weaker, even with those who identify as Jews by religion versus primarily by culture and heritage. Even among Jews who identify by religion, more than half (55 percent) say being Jewish is mainly a matter of ancestry and culture, and two-thirds say it is not necessary to believe in God in order to be Jewish. When planners review this data, they come to understand that the challenges their synagogues are facing are not unique to them but reflect broader trends in American Jewry.

c. Other Studies. There are a host of books and articles that talk about Jewish identity and the needs and wants of prospective members. I find the data from the book *The Jew Within* (Eisen and Cohen 2000) very helpful. The insights from Dr. Jack Wertheimer's book on Conservative Jews, *Jews in the Center* (2000), shed light on different types of Jewish attitudes and practices. *Jewish Megatrends*, by Rabbi Sid Schwarz (2013), has several early chapters that paint an insightful portrait of the trends, factors, and forces that are impacting our congregations.

Leaders are always asking me about the 70 percent of their members who are only minimally engaged. You can do surveys and polls, but the disengaged don't often participate. One good place to start is sociological studies of typical congregational members. The Synagogue Studies Institute has a website with many helpful studies and stories (www.synagoguestudies.org). These portraits are, in my experience, very descriptive of many of the attitudes and beliefs I encounter. You might consider starting from these overviews and developing some ideas. Next drill down to the unique issues of your congregation. By analyzing a book or study's portrait of attitudes toward worship or ritual practice, you can ask how your congregation's attitudes compare. You can then make some hypotheses about your community that you can test in the planning process.

Challenge #2: Leaders Get the Wrong Data

Lawrence Butler identifies challenges of data management for nonprofit boards: being overloaded with data, having inappropriate data, having anecdotal data, and lacking the relevant context for the data (Butler 2000, 170). Synagogues sometimes don't have good data on their finances or membership numbers and simply can't do a five- or ten-year lookback.

Some ways leaders can get the wrong data include the following.

a. Data Overload. Many synagogue database programs gather data about members' interests. Leaders think that if you run a report from the database, you can find all the information you need about their members. However, data gathered when a member joins may not be accurate years later.

The Misguided Mailing

One executive director was proud that he had gathered data and created a list of over one hundred members who he thought would be interested in a social action program. He then sent out a mailer to them about the program. I asked him if it had turned up anything. He said "very little." The data was not current; it had come from the membership applications they filled out in haste when they joined. This data had not been filtered. He needed to know *who was very interested and passionate about* social action *now*. What he got were lots of names of people who, at some point, had some interest in social action. Not surprising that they didn't show up.

SVP CASE

b. Inappropriate Data. We have all watched the scene when the treasurer brings in detailed budget reports and presents them to the board. The treasurer dumps the spreadsheets with their eight-point font on the table, and people's eyes roll. This is an example of inappropriate data. It is too dense; it is in a format that is alien to many; and it is in a font that is hard to read. I recommend instead creating one-page executive summaries that highlight some of the key variances and encourage the finance team to offer an explanation. Nonprofits are under pressure to be more transparent. They are asked to keep stakeholders and members informed. Even when they want to do this, they often lack a way to make the most important information user friendly, accessible, and understood.

If the budget process is working, the board probably doesn't need to see all the background at each meeting. If there is an emerging issue of great importance, it should be highlighted (for example, in a large font) in a helpful manner so that participants can give the report the respect it deserves. I call this "managing by exception."

When it is time to approve the whole budget, there should be an executive summary and guide to identify the key critical issues. That kind of information is helpful and appropriate and less likely to overwhelm the leadership.

c. Anecdotal Data. In the absence of actual data, planning leaders often get anecdotes from various people. I once worked with a day school that was concerned about losses in enrollment. One leader insisted that people were leaving because the school was too religious. After I reviewed exit interviews, I found that 60 percent of families left because they moved out of the area. Another 20 percent left because of financial considerations. The remainder left because the school was too religious or not religious enough. So we suggest you commit to getting those exit interviews before you make the wrong assumptions. Anecdotal data can be helpful if it points you in the direction of ideas to explore and validate.

SVP CASE

Exit Interviews: Why Do They Leave?

One synagogue was complaining about how difficult it was to obtain exit interviews. They said, "We can't get them." "Why bother? Will they ever really tell us the truth?" "They are leaving. They won't take the time." I knew there was some truth in this. Some members had bad experiences with exit interviews. In my experience as a marketer, however, I knew that if I was persistent and resourceful, I could get invaluable information. The group eventually conceded that the data was important. They realized that they had assigned this delicate task to a member who had limited interpersonal skills and sounded angry on the phone. It made those who had left the synagogue feel defensive. The board realized that they had assigned critically important work to the wrong person.

d. Data without Context. Leaders are quick to talk about membership trends. If they are declining, they will express anxiety about the future and look to me for some inspiring strategies. It is therefore very important for me to understand the "real numbers." After review, it is not uncommon to find a recent year with a significant (10 percent or more) decline in membership. I ask, what happened here? Did the president offend people in the High Holiday appeal? Often what has happened is that a new membership chair or executive director reviewed the membership rolls and found a significant number that had not paid in many years. They then do what most good businesspeople do. They write off the dues and take those people off the membership rolls to provide a more accurate picture of membership. There is usually a great deal of emotion surrounding this adjustment. "What happened to membership?" they cry.

One leader described the prior executive director as simply not having a grip on the numbers. Another past president confided that he felt the executive director knew the numbers were not accurate but was trying to be sensitive to the rabbi who got upset when a member left. This is what Susan Shevitz means when she calls synagogue organizations "non-rational" (1995). Many essential management facts are covered over to avoid the emotional pain of the truth.

Another congregation on the east coast claimed to be a congregation of over 700 members. When we reviewed their numbers, they only had 375 households who were paying full dues. They had 100 families who had children in the preschool and got free membership in the hope that they would eventually join. Perhaps 25 percent of them went on to join later. There were many paying minimum dues. The problem was that they were staffing for a congregation of 700 households and they really were only about 400 households. It was no wonder they were having financial problems.

If you look at data without reference to the larger congregational context, you might think you are doing better or worse than you really are.

e. Leaders Get Survey Data They Can't Manage. We will discuss the pros and cons of surveys in chapter 9. Surveys often raise congregational expectations. Members have shared some things they are concerned about, and they want to know if the leadership is going to take action. Synagogue staff have limited capacity, and surveys welcome a sea of hopes without a filter. Leaders then have to explain why they chose to work on some things and not others.

Let's Just Send Out a Survey

Every year, we get calls from leaders who just want us to send them a survey. We ask them some clarifying questions. "Do you have a planning committee?" "What will you do with the data?" "Will you create task forces to follow up?" The usual response is that they have not discussed any of those things. We then explain why we will not be sending them a survey. It is hard enough to execute any kind of planning process. When you launch a survey without a planning team or a process to follow up, it makes success very unlikely, and more importantly, it gives the planners and the planning process a bad name, which makes future planning even more difficult.

Challenge #3: Leaders Fail to Make the Connection to Their Community

Leaders often fail to connect data and consider possible implications. When we discuss the forces affecting congregations, I ask leaders to identify if these forces are having a low, medium, or high impact on the congregation.

What Helps

1. Learning about Your Congregation and Others

We suggest you have the steering committee explore their attitudes about the congregation using the Thriving Congregations Assessment (TCA). Obviously your leadership assessments are subjective. It is not easy to assess your performance or that of others, but you must try. Once you have the results of the TCA, you can later use surveys and focus groups to compare and contrast what leaders think versus what the congregation thinks. The truth is usually somewhere in between.

Your knowledge of other congregations may be sketchy, but you are not without sources of information. You and your planning team have friends and family members at these other congregations. They may have visited them for holidays and lifecycle events. Though you may be reluctant to compare your congregation to others, this is a healthy exercise and always provides some valuable insights.

2. Learning about the Affiliation Process—Data Needed

Leaders need to gather data on how members experience the congregation at the various stages of affiliation. This data contributes to developing a membership strategy.

Affiliation Stage: Prospects' Needs	Welcoming: What Leaders Should Do	What Data Should We Gather?
Seek: Prospects are looking to meet basic needs.	**Build Awareness:** Make prospects aware of values, identity, and programs (by advertising, special events, open houses, etc.).	What is our brand image in the community?
Test: Prospects visit the congregation, talk to members, and observe and interact with clergy.	**Welcome:** Every member should be an ambassador. Ushers are trained to greet properly. Demonstrate that we welcome new members and care about them.	What are members' first impressions? What do they say to office staff, educators, clergy, or welcoming committee members?
Return: They come back; they follow up with questions.	**Follow Up:** We need to assign someone to build on their interest and educate them about the congregation.	What are the key decision-making criteria of our prospects? Why do they join? What makes them reluctant?
Join: They sign up.	**Engage:** Welcoming team helps connect them to other groups and individuals. Mentors plan new member dinners.	What data do we gather when they join? Who uses the data? What is done with the data?
Deepen: They hope to become included. They reflect on whether the congregational experience was what they hoped it would be.	**Monitor and Maintain:** Membership committee tracks their progress in the first year to make sure they find their home in the congregation.	What percent get a follow-up letter or a call? Go to new member Shabbat? Connect with a mentor? Join a group? Get involved in committees or projects in the first two years?

It is very important to map out the experience of members and prospective members at each stage in their journey. (See chapter 15 on design thinking, which teaches planners how to gain a deeper understanding of the member experience.)

3. Learning About Your Prospective Members

An effective membership strategy involves both retaining current members and recruiting new members. You need to identify who are your most likely membership prospects. Who are the people in the community who would most benefit from joining your congregation? Who would best fit your culture? Let's say you have decided that young families are a demographic that you would like to do a better job of attracting to your congregation. How might you go about exploring a strategy to attract more of these families? One thing that helps is to develop a profile or persona of that person so you can visualize their needs. Let's play with this.

Exercise: Understanding the Young Family Persona

Who are they?

Parents are typically age thirty to forty with busy work schedules and very little discretionary time. Their children are in religious school and/or preschool and engaged in other extracurricular activities, including sports and performing arts. Money may be tight.

What do they say they want?

They say they want quality Jewish education. They are serious consumers and want to ensure that their children will gain a foundation in Jewish knowledge and basic skills. They don't want them to hate going to Hebrew school. They want them to feel a connection to their teacher and to their peers. They want the school and other parts of the synagogue to help them be successful and engage with other families like them. They want to see how Judaism, and their synagogue, creates a meaningful and rich life.

What is our unique appeal to them?

We are a medium-sized congregation, and we are known to have a top-rated religious school. Our grade sizes are fifteen to twenty children, so students will have the opportunity to make friends. We are close to where most of these families are buying homes. The public schools are excellent. We have beautiful and secure grounds. Some of the children in this segment have already participated in our summer camp program. We have a reputation of excellence with children.

What do we need to do to make them more aware?

Encourage more of them to come to our open house. Consider offering a second open house. Tell stories in Jewish media about our great family programs. Incent current members to bring friends. Do more to increase socialization of young families. Create small family groups (*chavurot*). Have them bring nonmembers to family programs.

What do we need to do to meet their expectations?

We need to continue to offer the same outstanding programs we have in the past. We need to increase the social networks in the congregation so families don't get lost.

4. Learning About Your Staff

The staff will play a central role in the SVP process. They will be one of the key stakeholder groups. They will also be asked to support task forces and committees in the implementation phase. It is very helpful to get staff input early in the process. The staff will be integral in helping planners understand how your programs provide the benefits that members want; they can also help define who the best prospects are. By meeting with the staff, we get background information about staff concerns that contributes to the design of the workshops and other planning processes.

5. Meeting with Key Committee Chairs

The planning process will create task forces later. One great place for planners to start is by interviewing committee chairs to find out what they have learned and what they are doing. The following are helpful interview questions.

Committee Interviews

Trends: Please let us know about the external trends that are impacting your work, such as changes in demographics of the area, new programs in the community, etc. Are there any changes in competitors or developments with possible partners?

Facts: What are the most important internal organizational facts we should know about your committee's area of concern (for example, attendance, enrollment, program satisfaction, effectiveness)?

Goals Last Year: What were the three most important goals you had for last year? Did you achieve them? What worked well? What could have been even better?

Goals This Year: What are your three goals for this year?

Support: How can the steering committee and synagogue leadership help you be more successful?

Committee interviews give planners an early indication of the key issues in the congregation. They also reassure the volunteers and staff working on the committee that their past work will be honored. They will have a "voice if not a veto" in the work to come. Some will be asked to be on task forces so that committee knowledge and experience can be utilized.

6. Empathic Listening and Community Conversations (See Chapter 10)

Empathic leaders observe synagogue behavior. They might observe members in worship services. When do they arrive, and when do they leave? When do they read or sing? When are they silent? When do they seem bored, and when do they seem most alive and engaged? From these observations, planners might develop some working ideas about increasing member engagement in the congregation. They could test these in small groups or use their insights in designing a future worship survey. Many SVP workshop exercises are designed to help leaders capture these insights. We explore how task forces can explore the member experience in chapter 15 on design thinking.

In your community conversations (chapter 10), you will ask current members when they have felt most connected to the congregation. You will ask them how we could build on these positive experiences, and you will seek specific suggestions for new programs and solicit information on what barriers they may see to deeper engagement.

7. Timelines: Effectively Telling a Story

A powerful vehicle for sharing data is the timeline. I have had some planning congregations list twenty years of membership and enrollment information and financial and fundraising results. This is particularly helpful with congregations that have avoided hard truths.

Seeing the Big Picture

One congregation had seen membership spike up and then go down several times over twenty years. They came to planning with great anxiety. Once the data was on the wall they realized why they were so ambivalent. They were not sure what had caused the swings or what the next trend would be. I helped them explore what had happened at each stage of their complex history. They were then able to have a better discussion about whether to scale up or scale down. It is pretty hard to miss the big picture when it covers fifteen feet of wall space.

Getting Started: Determining What Data Is Available

The president and the planning chairs are asked to review the Fact Book worksheet (see appendix resource 2). The goal is to identify the data you have and put it into user-friendly form. You also want to decide what other data might be useful. If there was a worship survey, can you find it? If you had some focus groups, can you obtain the results? Some data may take more effort to generate. The executive director can help planners understand how much effort is involved in getting each item on the list. Most synagogues do not have an abundance of staff. They need to prioritize their data-gathering efforts. If there is something that you feel is essential, you can explore whether you want to invest the time and energy to gather and organize the data.

Conclusion

We discussed the creation of the data gathering team in chapter 7. We have argued that leaders can be developed by doing more leadership-oriented tasks. One of the most important planning skills is determining the various kinds of data needed. Data gathering encourages leaders to ask tough questions about what really matters. With shared facts, they can begin to deal with the implications for the synagogue. These debates will lay the foundation for future strategies.

Questions for Reflection

1. What is the most important data that you need?
2. What would it help you do?
3. Choose one critical area. How might you go about gathering this data?

Chapter 9
Congregational Surveys

The biblical spies are tasked with surveying the land and coming back to describe the situation. We want our planners to gather the facts and hold off on debating the implications. The data-gathering team is tasked with using different data collection tools to understand the congregational situation.

If the team chooses to do a congregational survey, they need to communicate to the congregation the goals of the survey and how the data will be used. They also need to speak about how the survey reflects the congregation's values and why their participation is important (see the model letter in the appendix).

Benefits of a Survey

- Engages the larger membership community in the process of planning. Nobody is excluded. Everyone has the opportunity to share their views.
- Increases *transparency*. Lets the congregation know that a planning process is underway.
- Shows that you value congregational input.
- *Harvests specific ideas* that can be turned into short-term wins.
- Helps *inform evolving situation analysis*. Allows the team to create SWOT (strengths, weaknesses, opportunities, threats) 2.0 with input from the survey.
- Allows us to test some hypotheses.

Testing Hypotheses

Most leaders have some knowledge about the synagogue situation and its challenges. In the early stages of the process planners get new information from the Thriving Congregations Assessment, the fact book, and committee interviews. The planning process is a way for leaders to test some of the assumptions they have about the synagogue and its future.

Issue: Connection

- Leaders may feel the clergy and members reach out in times of need. Does the congregation feel the same way?
- Leaders may feel that members' talents and interests are known. Do members agree?

Issue: Communications

The survey can help us test our hypotheses about our communications.

- Do they know our vision?
- Do they understand our financial situation?
- Do they understand the volunteer opportunities that exist?
- Do they think we are transparent about our finances and decision making?

Challenges of Surveys

While there are some significant benefits of doing a survey, there are also some real limitations in the process.

1. Poor Predictors of Participation

In the twenty-first century members have little discretionary time and many competing interests. The things that they identify as of moderate interest may actually translate into a "no show."

Surveys can tell us something about members' past behavior. Have they volunteered in the past? Have they attended the family seder? Surveys, in my experience, are not good at predicting whether people will attend in the future or whether they will support a new program. Will they come to a book club on Tuesday? Would they go on a holiday retreat? Marketers are often tricked by focus groups that suggest that they like a product. When it gets to the shelf, people walk by. Members may say they have some interest but they seldom go to anything unless they are "very interested."

2. Raised Expectations

Surveys can produce anxiety for staff. Once the "great survey" is in, there is pressure to respond to the data. "Rabbi, we spent all of this money on research, and now we must show that we can respond." The rabbi looks at the programming ideas that are listed in the great "data dump" and asks, "What should I do with this data? We have the same staff as last year. How do I address all these additional requests?"

We get requests every year from leaders who just want us to send them survey questions. We resist because without a steering committee and a careful set of planning steps planning data may not be used properly. Expectations may not be met, and planning may get a bad name.

3. Key Segments Don't Choose to Participate

Based on our experience, 25 to 35 percent of households will respond to the survey. There are always a few outliers at both ends of participation. What we see consistently is that the survey is completed by the more engaged and longstanding members. We also see that most respondents tend to be older. How do we get younger members to respond? How do we hear the voices of the less engaged?

4. People Don't Know What They Want

Steve Jobs of Apple argued that customers often don't know what they need. He looked at how people lived and imagined things they had not even thought of. Henry Ford famously said that if he had asked consumers what they wanted, they would have said, "a faster horse." If you read the typical responses to our survey question "If you could wave a magic wand, what one thing would you want the synagogue to change?" you will find comments like, "make services more participatory," "make the congregation more welcoming," or "help us feel connected." They don't tell us how to invite members to share personal stories, wear name tags, or create a buddy system. Most members don't know of the innovative things other congregations are doing. Even if they have experienced a program somewhere, they may not recall the experience when completing a survey. They may say they want shorter services, but they don't imagine creating multiple service options that might include hiking and Torah study. They just don't know enough! If we want to probe our members' needs and get closer to what they might want, we need to look to our community conversation focus group process (chapter 10).

5. Findings May Not Be Actionable

Many times the data cannot easily be acted upon. Some members may want a very short service that the congregation cannot accept. The rabbi is not willing or able to cut major sections of the traditional liturgy. While others may want multiple services, the congregation may not have staff to manage them. Some may want improvement in the facility, but when the leadership comes back with higher dues, a building fund, or other sacrifices, that desire may become less urgent.

6. Poor Survey Communication Gives Planning a Bad Name

When the planning team is not able to explain how they are using the survey data, the congregation may be confused or skeptical. When administering the survey, the planning team needs to be explicit about the purpose of the survey and how/when the information will be shared and used.

Conducting the Survey: Key Elements

The survey explores key categories of the synagogue experience (see appendix resource 4).

- Who we are: demographics (consider listing one question below)
- Shared vision and direction
- Community connection
- Community inclusion
- Leadership capacity
- Unmet needs
- Things to change

Prelaunch Communication

- Explain the context (where you are in the planning process, what has been done to date)
- Indicate how long the survey will take to complete (10 minutes)
- Indicate the timeframe for completing the survey (three weeks, provide deadline)
- Responses will be anonymous: no tracking of email addresses
- Explain how the data will be used. An executive summary will be made available to help develop a plan. Highlights will be shared with the board, staff, and congregation.

We offer a model letter in the appendix as a guide (see appendix resource 5). It frames the message:

- We need your participation
- Survey reflects our core values of participation and democracy
- Need your talent and gifts

What Helps?: Promote and Keep Communications Coming

- Be creative
- Put in a call to action: Please take this survey!
- Put a poster in the foyer: We need to hear your voice!
- Review the process in religious school and teen groups: Ask them to ask their parents about it
- Pass out stickers (like you get when you vote) that say, "I completed the survey. My voice was heard!"
- Have leaders wear a name tag that says, "Ask me about the survey"

In all these ways you will be communicating that this planning process matters to you and is important for the congregation.

Data Analysis: Summarize Findings in a User-Friendly Way

- The data-gathering team needs to create and share an executive summary. This can be in narrative form or a PowerPoint slide deck. See chapter 12.
- Use it for board briefing
- Use it for town hall meetings

Chapter 10
Community Conversations

As we discussed in chapter 9, surveys can be useful. They allow every member of the congregation the opportunity to be heard. All they need to do is sit at home and take ten minutes to respond to the brief questionnaire.

Community conversations (CCs) can offer great insights but they require more energy. For someone to participate in a CC, they must RSVP in advance, show up at a specific time on a specific day, and commit to spend ninety minutes of their time. When people step forward to participate in CCs, we can see who has the energy to actually drive new ideas. We see who might be a potential task force member. We cannot cross into the Promised Land if we don't have some committed people in the procession.

> We created a process that we will turn to time and again for getting to know our members, and in doing so we trained our leadership in an important skill. (Rabbi Joshua Davidson, Temple Beth El, Northern Westchester)

CCs help gather information about what energizes people and gets them engaged. They can also help us identify some of the barriers to engagement. They can help identify who is passionate about particular topics and who might have the energy and the personality to help engage others.

The CC model is scripted using the language of appreciative inquiry in order to keep the discussion focused on the positive. With our carefully crafted questions and a skilled facilitator, these CCs will be a valuable way to get information from people who may not respond to a survey and to find and engage new leaders who may never have been involved previously.

The data that comes out of CCs is qualitative data, but it is just as critical, if not more critical, than your quantitative data. In fact, in smaller congregations, we often recommend that CCs be done instead of a survey. We will commonly recommend both a survey and CCs for larger congregations.

What Kinds of Community Conversations?

The data-gathering team chair needs to help the steering committee decide how many conversations to hold and whether they will be larger meetings open to all, smaller ones restricted to particular demographic groups (preschool families, families with teens, senior adults, empty nesters, Shabbat attendees, etc.), or groups related to specific areas of congregational life (for example, worship, Israel, learning, social justice).

CCs welcome a group of approximately eight to twelve people to spend about ninety minutes reflecting on key questions.

The planning objectives for these conversations are as follows:

- Obtain information about what encourages engagement in a specific demographic and/or interest group
- Collect information about what creates barriers to engagement
- Get a sense of the level of a member's interest in particular areas
- Learn who is passionate about particular topics
- Consider who might be willing to join task forces

Participants are asked two foundational questions designed to elicit a positive response:

- When have you been most engaged in the synagogue?
- How could we build on this? (Please be specific.)

From Blame to Contribution

The first question begins with appreciation for the synagogue. This is not an accident. We believe that we can get more creative and constructive energy by inviting people to think about what is working well. We then ask them to share ideas of how they might contribute to the solution.

This keeps the session from becoming a list of complaints. By avoiding "the gripe session" we make it much more manageable for a volunteer facilitator to manage this critical data gathering task.

Community Conversation: Types of Meetings

By topic:

- Member engagement
- Shabbat and ritual
- Learning and education
- Social justice
- Caring community
- Youth

By demographic segment:

- New members
- Preschool families
- Empty nesters
- Senior adults
- Saturday morning attendees

Logistics

Setup:

- Arrange seating at tables so that people can write
- Provide a copy of questionnaire for each participant
- Make sure to have extra pens for people to fill out questionnaires
- Adhesive flip no bleed chart paper to put on the wall, and markers
- Name tags and sign-in sheet
- Food

Volunteers needed:

- Skilled facilitator to lead discussion
- A host/recorder to take notes

Mount three Post-It sheets on a wall:

1. When were you most engaged?
2. How could we build on this experience for others?
3. One specific suggestion?

Conducting the Workshop

We designed the CCs to be a manageable task that any skilled facilitator can do. We want leaders to feel confident and hopeful. In our experience, facilitators have done these very successfully. Here is our annotated agenda to help you.

Annotated Agenda

(90 minutes)

Introductions: name, years in congregation (10 minutes)

Art of Asking (10 minutes)
The art of asking "primes the pump" and puts the issue of member engagement front and center. It gets participants ready to complete the questionnaire and share their thoughts openly.

Instructions:
- Pair up with someone you don't know very well.
- Each person has four minutes to respond to the following: *Think back to a time in your life when you felt really engaged in the congregation. What made you feel that way? How can we create more experiences like this for others?*
- After each person tells his/her story, the other person asks one clarifying question. The storyteller listens to the question but does not answer.
- Then switch roles.

Complete Questionnaire (10 minutes)
We ask people to reflect in pairs and then write before they engage in conversation with the larger group. We are trying to help them be reflective. We understand that not everyone is ready to share their thoughts openly from the beginning. We help get them started by asking them to

write answers to the two questions they discussed in the Art of Asking exercise. Note: I used the name Beth El for this exercise.

Name:
Email:

When have you <u>felt most connected</u> and engaged in the synagogue?

How can Beth El <u>create more experiences</u> like this for others? (Be very specific—no generalities.)

How might you be <u>able to help</u>?

When was the synagogue <u>at its best</u>?

What are some of the <u>barriers</u> to connection and engagement at Beth El?

If you could have us do <u>one thing to strengthen</u> Beth El, what would you suggest?

Sharing (45 minutes)

Data-Gathering Focus (Not a Debate)

This is a guided group interview, not a debate. Our primary interest is to gather data. Our most important documents are the questionnaires. We start out with a pairs exercise to get people thinking. The sharing process is to honor people's thoughts, not to debate them. We are giving people a chance to list their concerns, not litigate the issue or solve the problem. We are *not* giving people a "soapbox to stand on." This is like when we post some flip chart paper to hold ideas (a parking lot) in a board meeting to be considered at a future time. In this case the planning committee will review all of these concerns later.

Round One: 20 minutes

When have you felt most connected and engaged in the synagogue? Go around the room and welcome all comments (1 minute each).

Quick Debrief: What are some themes of these stories?

Round Two: 10 minutes
How might we build on these strengths to create more experiences like this for others?
Welcome volunteers to respond.

Round Three: 10 minutes
One specific suggestion?
Just list suggestions, no debate.

Emerging Themes: 10 minutes
When you think about all our comments what are some themes you heard?

Close: 5 minutes

The Recorder

We have the *questionnaire* that captures what the participants shared. Much of the conversation is getting them to *share* what they wrote for questions one and two. We post these on flip chart paper.

- The recorder does not also need to write these down. Details are all in their questionnaires.
- When we ask them to explore the themes that emerged, the *recorder needs to capture* these.

Facilitator Follow Up

- Facilitator scans questionnaires and sends with summary to the steering committee
- Facilitator puts questionnaire responses into a three-column summary table

    1. My great experience
    2. How to build on it to engage others
    3. One suggestion

- Facilitator writes up emerging themes from the recorder's notes of discussion
- Facilitator writes up "Barriers to Engagement"

Facilitator Debrief Form

They answer the following:

- What were five key themes you heard?
- What gave you hope?
- What was cause for concern?
- Who were some people who emerged as potential task force members?

Recruiting for Community Conversations

Now that the steering committee is ready to run the CCs, they will need to reach out to two kinds of people to help recruit participants. CC meeting participants agree to come for ninety minutes and share their thoughts. Stakeholders will be selected to represent the congregational segments that the leadership wants to know more about (that is, new members, longstanding members, etc.).

Finding Facilitators and Hosts

- All steering committee members should recruit some people and commit to attend at least one CC.
- The steering committee and data-gathering team should look to recruit people with facilitation skills to be trained to lead CCs.
- The steering committee and the data-gathering team should recruit people to host a CC at their home or at the synagogue. Hosts make calls, greet attendees, and can function as a recorder if needed.

Solicitation: Making the Call

The steering committee communications team will need to send a letter to the congregation to let them know that CCs are planned and participants are being sought. Some members will sign up in response to an email. Most will need to be solicited.

Why is direct solicitation necessary? I find that groups put a lot of energy into the invitation letter to attend these meetings. I often ask if they find that people respond to letters to attend a gala or to give to annual campaigns. They tell me that most of their success comes from phone calls or face-to-face solicitations.

Today's members are overwhelmed by junk mail. The direct mail letter or email blast is often simply background noise. While these communications may put the congregation on notice, it seldom produces many participants. The recruitment letter, however, does provide a good script to help the steering committee recruit participants by phone. The letter describes the key aims of the SVP process and announces that CCs will be held. This helps ensure that anyone who wants to participate in the process has the opportunity to do so.

Ultimately CC participants, like most leadership prospects, are recruited the old-fashioned way: one person-to-person encounter at a time. Leaders have to make the calls.

Overcoming Reluctance: Answering the Call

Most people do not like to solicit, but most will tell you that the primary reason they came to a volunteer program was because the right person asked them. SVP asks leaders to step forward to do the thing they know is pivotal in volunteer recruitment: to dial that number. The reality is recruitment is a necessary board skill. We need to recruit board members, committee volunteers, and members all the time. We need to get good at it.

God challenged Moses to lead the people out of Egypt. God challenged Joshua to lead the people into the Promised Land. What is God challenging today's leaders to do? My Christian colleagues call this experience of being challenged "the call." SVP was designed to gather leaders together so that they might find their congregation's "calling" and their own personal "call" to serve that mission. Leaders need to dial those numbers.

> What is God challenging today's leaders to do?

Calling with Hopefulness

Sample Recruitment Script
- I'm calling to invite you to participate in one of our community conversations.
- These interactive sessions are intended to gather your input about congregational life.
- Information gathered will be used to help us pinpoint areas of focus for our strategic planning process.
- Dates and times are . . .
- Please RSVP by . . .

Targeting

In my experience you can include almost anyone who wants to participate. You have the right to recruit more vigorously certain perspectives
that you need. The steering committee should look over the membership
list and brainstorm prospects.

The clergy and the entire professional staff are part of the solution.
Whom do they know? Who might be interested? They should review membership lists, benefactor lists, school parent lists, etc. These lists can jog
memories. Brainstorming surfaces some wonderful assets. It's worth it.
You can do it! Sources of CC meeting recruits and stakeholders include:

- Contacts from steering committee members
- Contacts from staff
- Those who respond to congregational letter
- Contact suggested by hosts

Group Size

Ideally, we are looking for eight to twelve people per group. I have had
groups as large as twenty, but it takes longer to hear from everyone. We
can invite a large group of people to a meeting on a Sunday. If we get forty
RSVPs we will need to have three facilitators.

Tracking the Recruitment

I suggest the steering committee chairs create a tracking form for all
groups. Consider these key questions while tracking recruitment efforts:

- Are we on schedule to recruit stakeholders so we can start the first
  workshop?
- Have we checked for duplications? We want to avoid having the
  same person contacted by two solicitors.
- Can other steering committee members suggest names for under-
  subscribed groups?

Questions for Reflection

1. How did you get recruited as a volunteer? What made a difference?
2. Have you ever successfully recruited another person? Why were you successful?
3. If you were coaching a new solicitor, what would you tell him or her?

PART IV

Making Meaning of Information

Chapter 11

SWOT 1.0

Getting the Lay of the Land

(Use first at second steering committee meeting.)

At this point in the planning process, data gathering is well underway. The planning team has collected information for the fact book, they have begun to interview key committee chairs and stakeholders, and leaders have completed the Thriving Congregations Assessment (TCA). A picture of the current situation is beginning to take shape and the SWOT exercise will capture the planning leaders' first thoughts.

In the second planning committee workshop we invite planners to report on the progress of teams and engage in this SWOT exercise. In this meeting we do an initial SWOT exercise that will allow them to look at the congregation's strengths, weaknesses, opportunities, and threats.

Wisdom from the Tradition

In the biblical story of the spies, we observe the struggle of collecting and evaluating data.

The Israelites were very much aware of the goal to enter the Promised Land, but they were worried about entering an unknown land and asked Moses if they could send spies who would bring back information that would help them conquer the land. Moses (begrudgingly) approved their request.

> When Moses sent them [the spies] to scout the land of Canaan, he said to them, "Go up there into the Negev and on into the hill country, and see what kind of country it is. Are the people who dwell in it strong or weak, few or many? Is the land in which they dwell

113

good or bad? Are the towns they live in open or fortified? Is the soil rich or poor? Is it wooded or not? And take pains to bring back some of the fruit of the land." (Numbers 13:17–20)

Too often, leaders are anxious about the future, rushing to judgment before they have fully reviewed the situation. In the case of the spies, their fear of the unknown made them accentuate their challenges rather than highlight their strengths.

We looked like grasshoppers to ourselves, and so we must have looked to them. (Numbers 13:33)

As leaders plan for the future, they need to keep two important concepts in mind. The first is that they need to be honest about their current situation. This is why we do extensive data collection of various types, in order to provide leaders with a shared set of facts and help them identify their critical issues. The conversations that emerge around this data will help the planning team thoughtfully evaluate and consider different strategies to address the issues.

Second, leaders must put forward a hopeful, positive vision of the future. This is the reason that when we do the SWOT exercise, we list the strengths first, allowing leaders to be hopeful about what's possible before they begin making lists of everything that is wrong. The rabbis were very critical of the spies, feeling that they did not accurately describe the whole situation.

In order to create a hopeful vision, leaders need to increase their capacity so they won't feel small and alone—like grasshoppers.

Sweet Fruits of the Land

Moses anticipates that leaders may be overwhelmed by the challenges. To help them see a more hopeful picture, he tells the spies to bring back physical evidence of what is possible.

And they came unto the valley of Eshcol, and cut down from thence a branch with one cluster of grapes, and they bore it upon a pole between two; they took also of the pomegranates, and of the figs. (Numbers 13:23)

As change occurs, leaders will get some immediate negative feedback from some. There is no way to move into the future and make everyone happy. As we pivot to focus on something new, some will feel that we are turning away from them and their priorities.

We have learned that most leaders fear change. They have anxiety about the impact of change on communal harmony. Change can be disruptive and difficult. Leaders are the ones who help us manage the anxiety of change in the short term, while holding up the sweet promise of the future that may be years ahead.

Strengths to Possibilities

It is natural for leaders to become anxious as the list of weaknesses and threats grows longer. When we complete the SWOT exercise, we want to end on a positive note. We do this by shifting the conversation to one about possibilities (see table). In this way, we are helping leaders bring back some of the "sweet fruit of the land."

Strengths	Possibilities
• Great facility: renovated five years ago	• Invite independent minyanim to use our facility. Increase business for caterer and social hall rental fees.
• Prime location near the JCC and major Jewish neighborhoods	
• Award-winning religious school with new computer lab	• Work to build Sunday as a facility day. Create more opportunities for online learning and small team projects that can be done offsite.
• Received awards for cooperative learning	

The SWOT Exercise

Goals of SWOT:

1. An Honest Assessment of the Current Situation
  • Identify what is working well so you can do more of it
  • Strengthen underdeveloped areas
  • Identify weaknesses and stop doing things that are hurting the congregation

2. Develop Foresight and Anticipate the Future
- Scan the environment to see future trends, factors, and forces that will impact the congregation
- Develop plans to take advantage of helpful opportunities and possibilities
- Minimize harmful external forces (threats)

Tips for SWOT:

1. **Look Beyond your Walls:** Consider opportunities to partner with others. Think about various community resources you might leverage (grants, local universities, etc.).

2. **Be Specific:** Where possible, provide supporting arguments for your claims. Don't just say "great location." Ask what it is about the location that makes it great. One possible response may be that it is a town where there is a large Jewish population, which can allow for partnerships and collaborations with other organizations.

3. **Get Objective Information:** Review the numbers from the fact book. Don't just assume that you know your membership or fundraising trends. Get the facts.

4. **Prune List:** Review your list of strengths and weaknesses and prioritize them.

5. **Connect Strengths to Possibilities:** Build on your strengths. How might you group multiple strengths and turn them into a new possibility?

6. **Plan to do Multiple SWOTs:** Keep updating the SWOT as your team learns more. The SWOT should serve as a receptacle for your data. As you gather more data, you will continue to revise your SWOT analysis.

Agenda for Second SC Meeting: SWOT Meeting (75 minutes)
Annotated Guide

Check In: Fifteen minutes

Text Study: Ten minutes

When Moses sent them [the spies] to scout the land of Canaan, he said to them, "Go up there into the Negev and on into the hill country, and see what kind of country it is. Are the people who dwell in it strong or weak, few or many? Is the land in which they dwell good or bad? Are the towns they live in open or fortified? Is the soil rich or poor? Is it wooded or not? And take pains to bring back some of the fruit of the land." (Numbers 13:17–20)

Talking Points

Moses asks the spies to bring back the fruit of the land to encourage a spirit of hopefulness.

He connects to the land, the soil, and the fruit in order to give the people a vision of their future, a taste of the next chapter in their journey.

Review Data: Twenty minutes

- Walk people through the Fact Book data.
- Share a summary of key learning from any interviews done to date.
- Reference the results from the Thriving Congregations Assessment.

Conduct the SWOT: Twenty minutes

The facilitator welcomes participants to do the following:

- List all internal strengths on one page
- List all internal weaknesses on a second page
- List all external opportunities on a third page
- List all external threats on a fourth page

Connect Strengths to Possibilities: Ten minutes

The facilitator invites participants to make the connection between current strengths and future possibilities. When leaders see the possibilities, they can taste some of the "sweet fruits" of what is possible.

Follow-Up Work After SWOT

Type up all the notes from the flip chart pages. Continue to update the SWOT as new information comes in.

Sample SWOT

Strengths (Left)
- Great facility: renovated five years ago
- Prime location near the JCC and major Jewish neighborhoods
- Award-winning religious school with new computer lab
- Received awards for cooperative learning

Weaknesses (Right)
- Congregation is aging
- Same active people involved in programs, not reaching most members
- More members on financial assistance

Opportunities (Left)
- More graduates of Jewish studies programs
- Impact of Ramah: Hillel, Birthright
- We can connect people on social media

Threats (Right)
- People are more self-sufficient and can build community on their own
- Jews are marrying later and delaying start of families
- Less oriented toward membership, less tribal
- Housing costs are rising and some families are having to move twenty minutes away; with traffic it can be thirty minutes
- Have to compete with children's sports on Sundays
- Those who live farther out have poor attendance

Conclusion

We do the SWOT analysis in the early stages of SVP to engage the planning committee. It is easy to facilitate and it creates a great early conversation. We give the planners some data to start with (fact book, TCA), but it is clearly communicated that we will need to create a new version of the SWOT after the data debrief. We will know more later.

Chapter 12
Data Debrief
Emerging Themes Workshop

By this point, we have spent months gathering data from numerous sources, and the results can be very overwhelming. Our challenge now is to cut through all of the "noise" and find ways to make meaning from all the data, to figure out what it is trying to tell us. We did some of this meaning making when we did our first SWOT (strengths, weaknesses, opportunities, threats) exercise in the second steering committee workshop (see chapter 11). At the end of this workshop, we will ask the steering committee to update the SWOT to reflect key themes from all of the new data.

We have collected facts about membership trends, attendance, and finance; we have the worksheets and notes from community conversations; we have notes from our committee interviews; and we have the executive summary of our congregational survey. How can the steering committee use its emerging insights to develop collective wisdom from all these sources of data? There are times when leaders need to really dig into the details, and there are times when we need to see the big picture. In the Emerging Themes workshop, our task is to get beyond the details and see the big picture. Let's see how some of the data might come together.

Contemporary Narrative: Sustainable Leadership

Let's look at a scene from a leadership discussion.

The nominating committee reports that they are having trouble finding people to agree to serve as president. The board's size is perceived as well above average. The board has forty-five members and the average among congregations is closer to thirty.

In interviews with the executive committee, they report that they are having trouble getting decisions made with so many people at the board meetings. There is a lot of distraction. It's exhausting managing all the different personalities and perspectives.

The Thriving Congregations Assessment shows that their leaders are not clear about the job descriptions of their committees, and few committees have goals.

Emerging Themes from This Discussion

- It would appear that this board needs to create an engaging leadership experience in order to attract and retain good leaders.
- Board size and composition are factors that need to be addressed and must be managed in order to create a positive experience for leaders.
- In order to be successful in getting people to step into leadership positions, there must be a systematic approach to recruit, train, and develop effective leaders, including developing clear goals and job descriptions for each leadership position.

Many lay leaders will rush to debate tactical issues such as whether the meeting should start at 7:30 or at 8:00, but we need to encourage them to think more strategically and see the bigger picture.

Youth Engagement

From the data:

- 65 percent felt developing youth was very important
- There seems to be difficulty retaining families post–bar mitzvah
- Big surprise: how many suggestions for a new youth program we got
- Major reason to stay as a member: programs for children
- Youth committee has some great ideas: see committee interview

Emerging critical issue:

- Engage teens and parents in planning

Possible task force:

- Youth engagement

Survey Debrief: Executive Summary

In order to facilitate a conversation about the survey, we have identified some basic issues that should be addressed. You are free to adjust this list as you see fit.

Steering Committee Tasks

- Review the executive summary of the congregational survey as a group.
- Request that each steering committee member complete a debrief worksheet.
- Steering committee names critical issues and strategic objectives in advance of vision builder meeting.

Survey Review

Here are key areas of data to review:
Who are we?

- What is the breakdown of how long people have been members of the congregation?
- What is the age breakdown of our membership?

Retention:

- Why do people say that they remain members?
- Are the reasons different for different subgroups (for example, by age or length of membership)?

Satisfaction:

- How satisfied are people overall?
- Are there some groups that are more satisfied than others?
- What percentage of members would strongly recommend the synagogue or the Shabbat service?
- Are there significant differences in Net Promoter Scores for newer members, or for people who attend regularly on Shabbat, or for families with children in the school?

A Note About Promoters

The members who say that they would *strongly recommend* the synagogue are what we call "promoters" (from Fred Reichheld's book *The Ultimate Question*). This is a major factor in synagogue vitality. If you want to inspire more people to be engaged or get the attention of prospects, you need raving fans who are passionate about your congregation, not people who say they are just "satisfied."

Community building:
- What are some areas where the sense of community is strong?
- What are some areas where the sense of community can be improved?

Specific suggestions:
- What did people say they would want to change?

Community conversations debrief:
- Review executive summary of all CC
- Welcome questions and comments

Data Debrief

Now that we have heard the reports on the community conversations and the congregational survey, it is time to make meaning of all that we have heard. We invite planners to collect their thoughts and take ten minutes to answer our questions.

Data Debrief and Emerging Themes
Workshop: Agenda (2–2.5 hours)

Welcome and Overview: 5 minutes
Data Debrief: 60 to 80 minutes
- Executive Summary of Survey: 20–30 minutes
- Questions and Comments: 10 minutes
- Executive Summary of Learning from Community Conversations: 20–30 minutes
- Questions and Comments: 10 minutes

Complete Debrief Journals: (see below) 10 minutes
Share Comments: 20 minutes

WORKSHOP

The facilitator asks three questions. The facilitator records statements on flip chart paper. They seek one response per person so everyone gets a chance to share.

Questions:
- What are emerging themes?
- What are most critical issues to work on?
- Name one shift the congregation needs to make.

Closing Thoughts: What are your Hopes?

Review Next Steps: 5 minutes
- Summarize the debrief journals
- List the *critical issues*

Use these notes to finalize the decisions about possible task force areas.

Complete Debrief Journal

Name:

1. What are the **three most important themes** that emerge for you as a planning leader?

2. What was **the most surprising** thing you learned from the data results?

3. The data identify various issues. What do you believe are the **three most critical issues** to focus on?

4. Please provide **one specific suggestion** that would really make a difference on your priority critical issue.

5. Please describe **one "shift"** that the congregation needs to make.
   We need to shift from_____ to_____
   _____.

6. What creates the most **concern for you**?

7. After reviewing the findings, **what gives you the most hope**?

Summary

After hearing summaries of the most critical themes that emerged from the congregational survey and community conversations, as well as from the fact book and the Thriving Congregations Assessment, we invited planners to make meaning, to create a narrative that can be used to describe the current state of affairs. In doing this they will be developing a common language as we move forward into the visioning phase and then to the task force phase. This critical step of summarizing and synthesizing all of this data and creating a narrative that planners can agree on is invaluable to the success of the planning process.

Chapter 13
Creating a Hopeful Forward-Looking Vision

Management scholars have argued that the two most important qualities of a leader are the ability to tell an honest story about the challenges of the present and the ability to create a hopeful, forward-looking vision of the future (Kouzes and Posner 2002).

The data-gathering phase of the planning process has helped us gather data about membership, finances, fundraising, and enrollment. It has tried to help us understand members' attitudes toward programs and services, thereby painting what we hope is *an accurate description of the current situation.*

The visioning phase challenges leaders to paint a *detailed portrait of the desired future.* It is aspirational. It describes what people would be doing, thinking, feeling, and saying if planning is successful. Both of these elements—the accurate description of the present and the hopeful vision of the future—are critical to planning. Unfortunately, the negative description of the situation often overshadows the hopeful vision.

It is only by holding the honest picture of the present in one hand and the detailed vision of the future in the other hand that we can begin to think about the strategic.

Staying Positive in Tough Times

The environment in which synagogues find themselves today has changed dramatically in the past half century (see chapter 3). It is important to recognize that many congregations facing these challenges are understandably concerned. Operating from a perspective of scarcity, they often compete with other congregations and organizations for members and resources rather than collaborate in order to create synergies and savings.

The Congregation That Could Not Vision

When we do a visioning exercise, we instruct leaders to share positive, aspirational statements that describe their desired future in detail. We ask them, "If we were successful, what would this community look like? What would people be doing, thinking, feeling, and learning?" When I was doing this work with one congregation, I got these kinds of responses:

- Kids wouldn't drop out of Hebrew school after their bar or bat mitzvah.
- Members would care more about Judaism and come to services more.
- Families wouldn't just act like consumers.
- The same people wouldn't always have to do everything.

Despite my prompt to give us positive, aspirational language, one negative comment led to another. These statements show us an example of a "problem saturated story." This kind of language and group dynamic reinforces a negative mindset and actually contributes to the difficulties that congregations are experiencing. So we find it useful to use language and techniques from the field of appreciative inquiry to shift the conversation away from complaints and critique and keep it focused on positive dream language.

Using the appreciative inquiry technique of "taking the positive opposite," I showed them how they can talk about the issue in a more hopeful way. The reframed comments look something like this:

- "I see people making time to go to services to support our mourners."
- "I envision new people stepping up to help make our community more vibrant."
- "I can see parents sitting in the library and studying Torah while their kids are in school."

We utilize the insights of appreciative inquiry to begin to transform pessimistic and critical attitudes into more positive ones. We have found that transforming a negative mindset based on scarcity to a more positive and optimistic one requires an effective reframing of issues and a different telling of the story.

A feeling of scarcity can set members against each other: old versus young, new members versus longstanding members, ritual conservatives versus liberals, etc. In these types of circumstances, when people don't know *what* went wrong, they often turn to *who* went wrong. Rabbis, lay leaders, Jewish organizational leaders, and others have all been blamed for the current state of affairs, much of which has little to do with any of them. We need to find ways to move away from the negativity, and the blaming that goes with it, in order to move forward.

We have discussed how Moses sends out twelve spies on a reconnaissance mission. When they return, ten of the twelve describe the Promised Land as full of obstacles. Only two spies saw the positive possibilities. Our Vision Builder workshop helps planners "taste the sweet fruits" so that they can move forward with hope and excitement for the possibilities of the future.

Helpful Tips for Visioning

The Vision Builder workshop teaches leaders how to do vision work so that they can inspire and lead their task force groups. The following are some helpful tips for creating an inspiring vision.

1. **Think of your Desired Future:** Most leaders are focused on the short term. We encourage them to think out three to five years, not three to five weeks.
2. **Facilitators Welcome All Dreams:** We want leaders to welcome new people and their new ideas. We use brainstorming to let ideas "bubble up."
3. **Start Anywhere:** Describe an aspiration or a dream and imagine a practice. Think of your synagogue at its best and then think how you could build on it. (Rabbi Harold Schulweis started with the need to help people who came to him for pastoral care. He then cast a vision for a Valley Beth Sholom Counseling Center.)
4. **Your Vision Must Inspire Your Leaders:** Your vision should shape the work of your task forces. We are not trying to create a tag line like "GE: We bring good things to life." We want a rich, detailed portrait of our aspirational future.
5. **Put a Frame Around It:** We want planners to focus on specific areas rather than the congregation overall. After the data-gathering phase we ask leaders to pick the focus areas for task forces (for example, leadership, learning, worship, community).

6. **Help Torah Speak to Your Vision:** During the journey it is help-ful to study Jewish texts that speak to core values that will shape your vision work. Find texts that inform your emerging vision. This book tries to do this. Make strategic planning a learning process.

7. **Let It Be Messy:** Plan to create multiple versions of the vision, that is, Vision 1.0, Vision 2.0, etc. Leave it in bullet phrases, don't wordsmith. We believe that visioning is an iterative process. You do not need to create it in one session.

8. **Make a PACT to Connect Vision and Reality:** Create supporting actions using our PACT goal format (see chapter 16) as an exercise to see if your vision can drive change.

9. **Be Mindful of Your Capacity:** Think about what resources (staff, volunteers, budget) would be required to bring your vision to life.

Vision Builder Workshop (150 Minutes)

Goals

The goals of this workshop are to do the following:

- Teach visioning as a foundational skill
- Create hopeful, forward-looking visions for specific focus areas of the congregation
- Move planners away from only looking at problems, gaps, and deficits
- Create energy that will inspire the work of the task forces

Workshop Preparations

Materials:

- Large easel pad with adhesive pages (3M Post-It pad works very well: need to be able to put up on walls, won't leak)
- Three pages for each of the four to seven groups
- Flip chart markers for each group
- Masking tape may be needed to help secure paper to the wall
- 3" × 5" index cards, one per person

Room Setup:

- Set up one round table for each focus area in a semicircle facing the front
- Place an easel or a tabletop flip chart on table; you can also use a nearby wall
- Put a sign on each table indicating which task force it is dedicated to
- Note that people will be standing for much of the vision exercise

Handouts:

- Brief summary of data highlights
- Most recent SWOT
- Latest version of mission statement

Assignments for Workshop:

- Steering committee member liaison to task force
- One staff assigned if available
- Assign staff, board, and steering committee members where you think they would be most helpful. They will come into the workshop and go to their assigned table.

Model Agenda

Welcome: 5 minutes
Overview of Process to Date: 5 minutes

- Explain the timeline of the planning process and how visioning fits into the bigger picture

Present Latest Version of the SWOT: 10 minutes
Text Study: Reflect on Importance of Vision: 10 minutes
We have participants read the text and then we ask them to describe the two leadership approaches.

Whenever Rabbi Hanina and Rabbi Hiyya were in a dispute, Rabbi Hanina would say to Rabbi Hiyya: "Would you really argue with me? If, Heaven forbid, the Torah were forgotten in Israel, I would restore it by my argumentative powers."

To the question of what he would do if the Torah was forgotten, Rabbi Hiyya replied: "What would I do? I'd go out and sow flax seeds; from the flax plants, I would make nets; with the nets, I would trap deer, whose flesh I would give to orphans, and with whose skins I would prepare parchment for scrolls, upon which I would write the Five Books of Moses. Then I would go to a town with no teachers, and teach the Five Books to five children, and the six orders of the Mishna to six other children.

Participants see that the two rabbis represent very different visions of how to lead and provide direction to the community.

Focus on Strengths: 15 minutes

In order to set the stage for the vision exercise, we help the group reflect on their strengths.

1. We list the strengths from the SWOT analysis that are derived from data from the Thriving Congregations Assessment, the survey, and the conversations in column one.
2. We then welcome the group to list other strengths in column two.
3. In column three we welcome leaders to think of other strengths or assets to explore in the community.

This process "primes the pump" and helps leaders realize that they have greater capacity than they might think. We believe that dreaming about the future is best done from a place of abundance rather than scarcity.

(1) Thriving Now (from TCA and other data)	(2) Add More Strengths	(3) Add Community Strengths
Prework: scribed on sheet in advance	Facilitator solicits	Facilitator solicits

Whole Group: Leadership Vision: 20 minutes
The facilitator leads the group in building a vision for the focus area of *leadership.*

- We start with the entire group standing before a wall of flip chart paper: three pieces.
- We choose one topic to start with: "Leadership."

Examples of Strengths to Build On:

- Highly dedicated to the congregation
- Generous with their financial support
- They truly love the synagogue

Review Brainstorming Rules
Before we start the brainstorming for the leadership vision, we review the rules of brainstorming:

- All ideas count
- Make sure as many people as possible get a chance to share
- No debate
- Just say what you believe, don't argue with others
- Speak of the ideal future, don't solve problems
- Think out three to five years
- Talk in dream vision aspirational language

Examples of Dream Language
Encourage them to use words like

- We would dream that . . .
- We would hope to . . .
- I imagine that . . .
- I imagine we would hear . . .
- I envision that people would feel . . .

Welcome Responses:

- Invite them to write down at least one dream on a card.
- Then ask them to share what they wrote on the cards.
- Try to hear from all of "the willing" before others speak twice.
- After this first round, people can share whatever comes to mind, no cards necessary.

Small Group Work: Ritual Worship Example: 45 minutes

The larger group has been assigned to break out groups based on the various focus areas chosen by the steering committee after the data debrief. They are seated at the table with their assigned topic on the tent sign.

At the table is the proposed *task force chair from the steering committee and one designated board member to help facilitate.* There is also a *staff person* who will be working on this area.

They begin by doing a vision for their area. They simply follow the process that they just observed on leadership. Here is an example of what this might sound like for ritual/worship:

Appreciate Now: 10 minutes

- The facilitator welcomes people to share what they appreciate about worship. They can reflect on the synagogue's strengths in this area.
- A recorder writes these down after the facilitator repeats the statements.

Possible Statements of Strength and Appreciation:

- I appreciate that we still get a morning minyan.
- I like the way we have people call out names during mourners' kaddish.
- I love our melodies.

Visioning: New Aspirations: 20 minutes

- *I dream that adults would be able to find a tutor to help them feel more comfortable in our service.*
- *I can see people at a retreat center charging up their spiritual batteries.*
- *I hear the sounds of new melodies.*

List Tasks/Ground the Vision: A Few Specific Tasks: 15 minutes

- *Explore a Saturday morning learners' minyan*
- *Visit other congregations in the region for Shabbat services and report back*

Gallery Walk/Report Out: 3 + minutes for each group, 30 minutes

- The whole group walks over to each small group discussion area and stands in front of the group's statements on the vision map. (Some may choose to have the presentation at the front of the room with a microphone.)
- The group facilitator reads the *vision* statements.
- The group facilitator shares one *concrete goal or scenario.*
- Participants share their responses verbally or write on the wall.

Close/Thank You/Review of Next Steps/Evaluation: 5 minutes

- Leader will write up all notes
- Chairs will begin to recruit for task forces

Chapter 14
All Task Force Workshop
Empowering Others

In this chapter we describe the process of welcoming new planning partners to join the steering committee for the task force phase of the process. What can we learn from our tradition about the transition of welcoming new leadership?

Joshua is part of a succession plan. God chooses him to follow Moses. Moses knows Joshua's nature. He sees that Joshua has courage and faith. He has the trait of alacrity: he has energy and zeal for the mission. Joshua is not afraid, like the other spies, to take on the challenges of the Promised Land. When the time comes, Moses lets him make some decisions. He puts his hands on him to pass the mantle of leadership. Moses places the spirit that is in him upon Joshua. Moses celebrates this transition in leadership in front of the whole community (Deut 31). He ritualizes the transition with the help of the priests.

Joshua has a successful transition and is able to step forward to the next chapter in his leadership. In contrast, in the book of Judges, there is little succession planning, and one successful leader is not followed by another. Chaos usually ensues.

The steering committee is like Moses. They have had a special responsibility to guide the planning process for the first six months. Now they have to welcome the task force chairs and empower others to take on leadership. The task force chairs have to recruit, orient, and train their new members. What can we learn from the successful handoff from Moses to Joshua?

- **Recruit:** Pick your task force chairs carefully. Consider which ones have the passions, interests, and gifts for each task force area. Match them with the right staff to support them. Have the chair

find a co-chair so that he/she can take the spirit that they have and
share it with a fresh leader.

- **Orient and Inspire:** Moses tells Joshua according to Rashi (Numbers 27:18) that he is "fortunate to have merited to lead" this mission. People have more energy for mission if they understand its
  purpose. Let them see the importance of the mission and their
  potential contribution.
- **Empower:** Moses lets Joshua make some decisions while Moses
  is still alive so the people would not say that Joshua "dared not
  raise his head" when Moses was in charge (Sifrei Pinchas 23). The
  tradition tells us that in his last days, Moses agrees to let Joshua
  teach him. The steering committee is going to give the task force
  an outline of things to consider (initial vision and tasks), but they
  should expect the task force to share their own ideas. Like Moses
  we want to give our mentees a chance to lead.
- **Recognize:** We could have just assigned people to a different
  subcommittee and let them go their own way. Why bring them all
  together? Moses understands the need to recognize his successor
  in front of the tribes (Deut 31). At the all task force meeting the
  steering committee, board, and staff are invited to welcome the
  new planners and support the beginning of their work. Like Moses
  we recognize and ritualize this transitional moment.

Task Force versus Committee

Let's compare the work of a planning task force to a standing committee
of the synagogue. Once you see the difference you will appreciate why
the task force usually cannot be composed of the same people who are
on the committee.

Committees
- Work is focused on short term
- Committee handles regular business
- They manage program details with the staff
- Work is ongoing and many members participate for years
- Utilizes experienced leaders

Task Forces

- Long-term: looking for strategies for three to five years out
- Vision: task forces look at what is possible over a longer period of time
- Possibility: they consider what they might do if they committed more resources to the new work
- Time limited: the committee leader may stay on for years, but we ask task forces to meet for three to four months
- Insist that core leaders join up with those outside the core to have new people that we call "fresh"

Composition: Who Is on the Task Force?

- Cochair: steering committee representative
- Cochair: non–steering committee representative
  - Increase leadership opportunities, share work
- Staff representative: helps ensure work gets done and has assigned tasks
  - Reports to lay chairs and "staff supervisor"
- Other members: four to eight people
  - Core—Experienced leaders and some members of the current committee
  - Fresh—Some new people who have shown talent and interest but are not part of the board or a committee

Tasks

- Review the initial vision for the task force (Vision 1.0). Build on it.
- Review the initial task list of things to explore and do.
- Review all data that relates to their area from the data-gathering phase.
- Continue to gather more information as needed.
- Develop strategies.
- Make a recommendation for action using the PACT goals template (later in the chapter).

A Critical Mass of Community Leadership

Seventy people go into Egypt with Jacob. This ensures the survival of the Jewish people. In the desert wandering, God, Moses, and Aaron are the top leaders. At Mount Sinai the seventy elders gather at the foot of the mountain. They will be tasked with helping disseminate the Torah learning. When we enter the rabbinic era, we get a rabbinic court of seventy judges called the Sanhedrin. They will translate God's vision into practical laws.

We began this process with the initial commitment of the rabbi, president, and planning chair. The leadership expands into a larger group that we symbolize with the number seventy. This larger community has the critical mass to represent the whole community and to be able to get things done.

Attendees

- The planning committee of ten to twelve
- The staff members working on task forces: four to seven
- The four to seven task forces with five to eight people each: twenty to fifty-six
- Interested board members who choose to participate

Total Participants: thirty-five to seventy+

Diagnosis and Dialogue

In our introduction we said that our method is a hybrid of "diagnostic" planning and "dialogic" planning. That sounds like a lot of academic jargon. What it means is that we start out with problem solving. In the data-gathering phase, we gather data and then identify the problems and challenges we face. We use this diagnostic approach to identify and prioritize the focus areas for the task forces.

In the visioning phase, the consultant and planning leaders step back to welcome the board and staff to dream and construct the future together. These new planning leaders become part of a larger conversation. Their emergence requires that the steering committee keep its thinking open and porous. Their ideas blend with the ideas of others. People begin to learn new things together. They find that they have more solutions than they imagined. They are not like an orthopedic surgeon, who acts as an expert, looking to diagnose a stress fracture. They are more like a therapist who invites the client to help construct their own future.

Now in the all task force meeting we use both diagnostic and dialogic techniques. In the orientation stage of the workshop we share the information and diagnoses we have developed to date. We then send the participants to the break-out sessions so they can begin dialogic conversation to construct initial plans.

Prework: Provide Hand Outs
- Fact book (optional)
- Executive summary of survey and community conversations: key learning
- SWOT
- Visions and tasks for each group (from Vision Builder workshop group breakout notes)

Room Layout:
- Place round tables in a semicircle facing front
- Put a sign on each table (Finance, Membership)
- Assign each person to a task force table
- Registration table: check people in and give name tags with table number

Presentation Tools:
- Projector and screen at front
- Laptop connection cord
- Easel with pad at front of room
- Portable microphone for sharing comments

Agenda (2–2.5 Hours)

Welcome/Review Process to Date/Steering Committee Chairs: 5 minutes
- Chairs describe the steps completed to date and the future steps to be completed

Orientation

Review Situation Analysis: 15 minutes
- Present executive summary of SVP congregational survey and conversations
- Review latest SWOT

Review Vision, Rabbi: 5 minutes
- Shares rabbinic perspective on emerging vision

Journal: Questions on Vision, Questions on SWOT, Share Later: 5 minutes

Presentation: 20 minutes

Review Strategic Purpose

Strategy: An overarching direction, not fully defined.

- Example: Make ritual services "more relational." Encourage people to share things about themselves (who they are praying for, who they are remembering).

Action: Provide specific concrete measurable action to put the strategy into action within a certain timeframe.

- Example: Rabbi to ask members to share who they are standing for at kaddish. Start within six months.

Example: Strategic Purpose

- Ensure a continuous pipeline of lay leadership: the nominating committee and/or a leadership development team constantly identifies, recruits, trains, and engages new volunteers and leaders to go from generation to generation.
- 50 minutes

Engagement

Group Work: Engage: 60 minutes

Introductions: 15 minutes

- All members complete task force member profile
- Background
- Interests
- One strength to contribute
- All members take two minutes to share

Vision: 15 minutes

- Review notes from Vision Builder workshop, Vision 1.0
- Share some additional vision statements for your task force

Task List: 25 minutes

- Review initial task lists
- Add additional tasks

Next Steps: 5 minutes
- Set date for next meeting
- Discuss tasks and start to assign areas to explore
- Have a recorder/secretary assigned to take notes

Report Out to Whole Group: 2 minutes each, 15 minutes
- A few vision statements
- Two tasks

Close

Agenda for Next Task Force Meeting (75–90 minutes)

Check In: 5 minutes
- Reflections or questions on all task force training and meeting

Review Task Force Vision: 5 minutes
- Review initial vision and consider additional dreams, comments

Review Fact Book and Survey/Executive Summary: 15 minutes
- Members share insights relative to their task force area
- What additional information do you need to do your work?

Do Initial SWOT for Area: 15 minutes
(Optional) Design Thinking: Begin to map out the *member experience you desire* (list, flow chart, pictures; see Chapter 15): 20 minutes
Review Task Force Assignments: 15 minutes
- Continue work started at all task force meeting. List tasks to do and make assignments to members.

Close: Set Next Task Force Meeting

Chapter 15
Using Design Thinking to Reimagine the Member Experience

According to Wikipedia, *design* can be defined as "the creation of a plan or convention for the construction of an object, system or measurable human interaction (as in architectural blueprints, engineering drawings, business processes, circuit diagrams, and sewing patterns)." Imagine any consumer product, and one thing you can be certain of is that it went through a design phase before it was brought to market.

If you consider how mobile phones have changed over the past twenty years, you will see the impact that designers have on a product. From the first large, clunky wireless handsets with one-inch screens and an external antenna to the flip phone, to the Blackberry, to the iPhone, corporate designers did research, held focus groups, and produced and tested prototypes, all to discover what people really wanted their personal cell phones to look like, feel like, and sound like before bringing new versions to market.

A Tool for Task Forces

People who are trained in design are taught to probe deeply into the hearts and minds of their target consumers, to ensure that they truly understand their practical and emotional needs. Who are they? What do they really value? What would make their lives better or happier? So what does any of this have to do with synagogue visioning and planning?

When we begin the planning process with a congregation, they usually have several problems they are trying to solve. Most of them are predictable: how to attract more members, how to better engage the members they have, how to build a stronger leadership "bench," how to raise more money, etc.

What if we could apply the approach that designers use in developing consumer products to help solve the challenges of the modern synagogue? We would have a new tool for task force leaders who are challenged with taking a fresh look at various aspects of the synagogue. Most task forces tend to focus on quick fixes and small problem-solving changes. Design thinking allows us to make some bigger and bolder explorations. In the end, task force recommendations should provide some bold ideas and concrete action items that set up some next steps. Design thinking will help you be *bold*.

Designing the Member Experience

In the case of synagogues, the "product" we are designing is *the member experience*. Let's consider this for a moment. What does it mean to *design* an experience? Obviously, this is a very different challenge than designing a consumer product like a mobile phone.

Let's begin by defining the synagogue member experience as *the sum of every interaction a member has with the synagogue or any of its official or unofficial representatives, whether that interaction is in person, on the website, on social media, by mail, email, or by phone.* Every single interaction has the potential to positively or negatively impact the way a person feels about the congregation—even bumping into the rabbi in the supermarket, running into the synagogue president at Hebrew school pickup, opening a piece of mail from the office, or checking the synagogue's website for information on an upcoming program can influence how a person experiences, and feels about, the congregation.

Obviously, not all of these things are completely within our control, but designing an experience means controlling all the elements that we *can* control, for example, the website, Facebook page, brochures, mailings, email blasts, the atmosphere in the office, what the lobby looks like, what the worship services are like (as well as the food that is served after services), how special events are run, the atmosphere in the preschool and religious school, etc. In order to design a better member experience, we need to do so consistently across all of these touchpoints.

Empathic Listening

In design thinking, the first thing we need to do is learn everything we possibly can about the people for whom we are designing the experience. We do that by listening empathically, showing authentic curiosity, probing, and trying to understand people's real wants, needs, and values, whether or not they are actually able to articulate them. Let's look at a couple of examples.

Case #1: The Millennial Who Just Moved into the Neighborhood

Imagine that you are a member of a congregation's strategic planning committee. In doing your initial data gathering, you learn that there is a sizable group of young Jewish adults who recently moved into the neighborhood when a large high-tech company relocated to the community.

One member of the planning committee says that she recently met one of these young adults and would be happy to reach out. She arranges to meet the young man for coffee. She listens empathically (and does not get defensive) as he talks about how little interest he has in traditional synagogue life with all of its rules and red tape and how he really just wants to get together with other Jews his own age and celebrate holidays, maybe discuss Israeli politics, travel to places of Jewish interest, or go to a Jewish music concert. She listens to his hopes and dreams about what he is looking for in a career, in a potential life partner, and in a social life.

Case #2: The Disengaged Longtime Member

Now imagine that you belong to a congregation founded a generation ago by young Jewish families who were looking for preschool and religious school for their kids. Those founders are now mostly in their fifties, and their kids are out of the house. Though these folks were once very active, you know that many of them have now disengaged entirely from the congregation. They don't come to services anymore, they no longer volunteer, and they rarely come to special programs and events. Someone from the strategic planning committee is assigned to interview some of these folks. She listens attentively as member after member tells a similar story of feeling increasingly less connected to the congregation. They talk about knowing fewer and fewer of the "newcomers," of not feeling like the rabbi knows them, of not being acknowledged for their contributions as founders of the synagogue, and of feeling like the only people that matter to the leadership are the young families.

It is important to remember that when we are talking about the member experience, the *only* thing that matters is the member's perception. In this case perception is, quite literally, reality.

It doesn't matter whether the leadership spends the same amount of time working with empty nesters as they do with young families. If the empty nesters are feeling excluded, that *is* their experience and it needs to be taken seriously.

Designing Something New

Once we feel that we have a deep understanding of the people for whom we are designing the experience and we know the problems we are trying to solve (remember that we are talking about *their* problems, not *ours*), we can begin brainstorming ideas. To do this with a design mindset it is critical that our team be made up of a diverse group of individuals with different approaches and backgrounds—someone who belongs to our target population, someone who is an "outside the box" thinker, and someone with a business sensibility would be a good start—with the goal of designing a new, holistic, member-centered experience that meets our target population's needs and engages their emotions. This is where we want to be bold and think big. What we are trying to do is intentionally design a set of member experiences across all touchpoints that addresses people's needs, appeals to their emotions, and exceeds their expectations. The more creative and innovative the ideas, the better! *Every single touchpoint is an opportunity to create something new*, and if we have business-oriented folks on our team, they will help us consider our capacity and stay within our budget.

Here is an example of an experience with a strong emotional impact. It is from John Deere (yes, the tractor people!), and it is the experience they designed for a new employee's first day:

Shortly after you accept the offer letter from John Deere, you get an email from a John Deere Friend. Let's call her Anika. She introduces herself and shares some of the basics: where to park, what the dress norms are, and so forth. She also tells you that she'll be waiting to greet you in the lobby at 9am on your first day.

When your first day comes, you park in the right place and make your way to the lobby, and there's Anika! You recognize her from her photo. She points to the flat-screen monitor in the lobby—it features a giant headline: "Welcome, Arjun!"

Anika shows you to your cubicle. There's a six-foot-tall banner set up next to it—it rises above the cubes to alert people that there's a new hire. People stop by over the course of the day to say hello to you. . . .

You notice you've already received your first email. It's from Sam Allen, the CEO of John Deere. In a short video, he talks a little bit about the company's mission: "to provide the food, shelter, and infrastructure that will be needed by the world's growing population." He closes by saying, "Enjoy the rest of your first day, and I hope you'll enjoy a long, successful, fulfilling career as part of the John Deere team . . ."

Now you notice there's a gift on your desk. It's a stainless steel replica of John Deere's original "self-polishing plow," created in 1837. An accompanying card explains why farmers loved it.

At midday, Anika collects you for a lunch off-site with a small group. They ask about your background and tell you about some of the projects they're working on. Later in the day, the department manager (your boss's boss) comes over and makes plans to have lunch with you the next week.

You leave the office that day thinking, I belong here. The work we're doing matters. And I matter to them. (Heath and Heath 2017)

It doesn't feel like much of a stretch to imagine designing a similar process for new members of a congregation. The new member receives a welcome letter from the rabbi via email, and then a phone call from a friendly member who is of a similar age or stage of life. The member tells the newcomer a bit about themselves, gives them some information about the congregation, offers to meet for coffee, and invites the new member to join them at an upcoming event. When the new member shows up for the event, their new friend is waiting for them in the lobby and introduces them to some friends, who perhaps follow up with a Shabbat lunch invitation.

Prototyping and "Failing Quickly"

In the world of design, the ability to quickly test new concepts, go back, make revisions, and try again is critical to the process. Because we are designing *experiences*, not *products*, let's think about what this kind of "prototyping" might look like.

This is the part of the process that may be the most challenging for synagogues, which tend to be conservative institutions that are not always used to being nimble or flexible. The idea of testing out different versions of a concept and going through multiple revisions may be foreign to the congregational culture. Yet that is exactly what design thinking is all about. We just need to acknowledge that this may be a significant culture change.

Now let's think about how we can visualize the new member experience described earlier. If we have someone on our team with some basic drawing skills, we could present this concept in the form of a storyboard. The first frame might be the new member (let's call him Yoni) getting the welcome letter from the rabbi. The second would be Yoni getting a phone call from his new friend (let's call her Ilana). The third frame would be Yoni and Ilana at a coffee shop. The next would be Yoni arriving in the synagogue lobby for an event and seeing Ilana, who introduces Yoni to her friends. You get the idea. A storyboard is a great way to illustrate this multistep process. If your team has people who are more comfortable acting than drawing, another option might be a presentation using role playing.

Once we've illustrated the process visually, it's time to test it out! Take your storyboard concept and try it with *one new member*. Choose one person who has just joined the synagogue and have the rabbi send her a welcome email. Find one member of the congregation with whom you think she would get along well and have her call and introduce herself and set up a time to meet for coffee. Train this member on how to connect with the new person and listen to her story and then ensure that she arranges to meet the newcomer at a program or event and introduces her to her friends. You will find pieces of your process that don't work the way you anticipated. Great! You failed! Now fix it and try again!

Conclusion

A design-focused approach based on authentic curiosity and empathic listening, followed by collaborative problem solving, experimentation, prototyping and testing, can be a real game changer in the synagogue world, with potentially transformative results. Not only does it have the capacity to create innovative models of every aspect of synagogue life, from membership recruitment and engagement, to ritual, education, and leadership development, but the process itself can help to build more relational communities by giving people more opportunities to tell their stories while teaching others to listen empathically, by building truly diverse collaborative teams to creatively address community challenges, and by learning to be brave enough to fail quickly in order to succeed.

In the context of synagogue visioning and planning, this kind of design approach can be invaluable. After you've done the Vision Builder workshop and imagined together what the future might look like for various areas of synagogue life (for example, leadership and governance, worship, education, social justice, youth engagement), have each group choose one or two specific ideas and make them real by sketching out a storyboard or a flow chart to illustrate how it will work in detailed steps.

During the task force phase, each task force can be empowered to reach out to members and potential members in their focus area and learn as much as possible about them: What do they need? What do they value? What would improve their lives? And then they can work to design member experiences to meet their needs. Just remember that what people say they want or need may in fact be different from what they actually want or need. As the inventor of the automobile, Henry Ford, famously said, if he had asked people what they wanted, they would have said a faster horse. This is why focus groups, community conversations, and one-on-one stakeholder interviews are so critical to our planning process. We encourage every congregation to have at least one task force give this a try. It's a foundational skill for the future.

Questions for Reflection

1. What is one challenge that you have as a congregation that you can imagine addressing using design thinking? (Try to frame the question like this: "How might we design a different kind of Shabbat experience?" or "How might we design a new religious education program that kids enjoy and that parents want to send their kids to?")

2. Who could you interview in order to probe deeply into the wants and needs of your target group?

3. How could you do a small experiment to test out one of your ideas?

Chapter 16
Priority-Setting Workshop

The priority-setting meeting is a time for celebrating the work of our task forces. Completing their recommendations is a major milestone on the planning path.

For this reason, it is important for everyone (steering committee members, task force chairs, president, senior staff) to come together to share their task force vision, strategic purpose, and recommended actions. It is the responsibility of the group as a whole to have a firm understanding of all the recommendations and be able to prioritize them. This is not a time for the group to redo the work of a task force but rather to ask clarifying questions and ensure that any hidden (or not hidden) issues are being addressed in the strategic plan for the future.

The Priority-Setting workshop is about making strategic choices of action that are within the synagogue's capacity and that fulfill the mission and vision of the congregation. There is a halachic concept of "*tafasta merubah lo tafasta, tafasta meuta tafasta*," which means "if you seize too much, you have seized nothing, but if you seize a little you have seized something."

The Priority-Setting workshop challenges the planners to be realistic about their capacity. If they are too ambitious and aspirational, the board will have a tough time actually doing the work in the implementation stage. It is relatively easy for a task force to dream up bold ideas, but that doesn't mean that the staff and lay leadership can actually do these things.

If planners are impatient, they may expect all of these initiatives to start in the first six months. We use the workshop to challenge leaders to spread out their work so some items are short term (within the next six months), some are medium term (seven to eighteen months), and some are longer term (eight months+). We want the leaders to consider bold ideas but to understand that things that take a change in culture (a new voluntary dues policy, a synagogue without walls outreach approach, a series of bold ritual innovations) may require long-term cultural change and need just small steps now.

As the text suggests, if we try to grasp all of this *now* we may not have the energy, focus, or capacity to do anything well. We need to choose wisely and not grasp for too much.

Annotated Guide

Prior to Priority-Setting Meeting

The task forces prepare reports (based on the SVP recommendations model template). These are included in each task force report:

Template Focus Area—Education

- Situation Analysis: Background and SWOT
- Mission and Vision: Discussion of how mission and vision connect to your task force area
- List Vision: Why is this task force work important?
- Strategic Purpose: Strategic rationale, the why and how to achieve the strategic objective (for example, engage whole family)
- Trackable ACT-ions: Action, capacity, time (for example, Monthly Family Education Sundays, Start January)

Strategic Purpose

Why are you recommending this action? We need to know why a specific recommendation is important. How will the recommendations advance the synagogue's mission? If we focus too much on very tactical action items, leaders may get lost in the details. Why should leaders accept the recommendation? What will success look like? How does it fulfill the synagogue vision, move us forward, and help the synagogue thrive?

During our first task force meeting, members wanted to respond to the information that had been discussed to date about the synagogue and its needs. They immediately began to list specific, concrete, suggested actions. At the next meeting we encouraged them to begin to clarify the rationale for those actions: "the why." One committee had seventeen actions. The final report created three major strategies and grouped the actions under these three. Each action had a rationale: the strategy to answer "why" you were recommending the action.

—Jeff Jacob, Sutton Place Synagogue 2014

Decision Criteria

How does one identify the most important issues to work on? What decision criteria should one use? We provide a list of factors to consider. Ultimately leaders need to think about the impact the recommendation will have on the congregation's ability to engage or grow membership, raise funds, or drive their mission.

Factors

- Increase Revenue: Will this recommendation bring in more revenue from a program or from the assets of our building and grounds (rents, usage fees, etc.)?
- Reduce Cost: Will this recommendation reduce our short-term and/or long-term costs?
- Reduce a Risk: Do we need to make our building safer? Do we need more insurance?
- Do we need to reduce financial risks?
- Develop a Donor: Will this initiative help us to cultivate a donor, develop more solicitors, or raise more funds?
- Promote a Value or Principle: Will this recommendation support an initiative we are already committed to fulfilling? For example, if we are committed to social justice, will hiring a part-time community organizer help identify what members care about?
- Build Our Brand: Will this recommendation be consistent with our brand and identity? Will it reinforce an attribute that is critical to our success, such as a new member engagement plan?

PACT Recommendation Template: Leadership

Strategic Recommendation: Strategic (P) Purpose (The Why)

All board members and committee chairs should feel that they are a part of a leadership team in which their individual interests, talents, and skills are known and are used for the overall benefit of the synagogue community as a whole.

Action (A) The What?	Capacity (C) The Who?	Time (T) The When?
Action: Build a board briefing book with all of the key information board members and committee leaders need. Develop a training session to provide both the information and the emotional connection of joining a leadership team.	**Who:** Development team **How much?** Binders, printing, office time (current staff) **Who:** Leadership task force chair and executive director **Complexity:** We have never done this. USCJ has both a model table of contents for the briefing book and a design for the training.	**Medium Term:** Six months

Codes for Plan Recommendations

There will be various details that support the recommendations. We encourage the task force report recommendations to be as detailed as they can. We suggest some shorthand codes to convey approximations in terms of cost, complexity, and time.

Cost (Ranges will vary according to congregation size.)

Example of a Cost Range

- $: minimal–under $1,000
- $$: $1,001–$4,999
- $$$: $5,000–$24,999
- $$$$: $25,000+

Complexity

Planners need to consider the complexity in terms of the implementation of the recommendations. Is the recommendation something they can do now, or is it something that they have never done or that few synagogues have succeeded in doing? Will it stir up conflict that will take great skill to mediate and manage, or is the recommendation an idea that has already been in discussion/formation for a while and will be easier to implement? Use the following scale to estimate the complexity of implementation to help the team discuss capacity:

- Basic: C
- Moderate: CC
- Complex: CCC
- Very complex: CCCC

Time

How soon can we implement this recommended strategy? The time is allied with the issue of complexity. Some recommendations are very technical; for example, we want to set up a Facebook page or add a program to our calendar to improve membership engagement. Other action items could take years; for example, developing a capital campaign and a building project. When we gather the diverse task forces that have operated independently, it is helpful for them to see the timelines that other groups are proposing for their recommendations. Leaders should be able to recognize that not all of these task force initiatives can be done at once, with limited staff and volunteer leadership.

Timeline Scale: ST, MT, LT

- Short Term (ST): zero to six months
- Medium Term (MT): seven to seventeen months
- Long Term (LT): eighteen + months

Collaboration between Task Forces

The steering committee needs to monitor the progress of the task forces and request interim reports. When they look at interim reports they may see challenges. Some task forces may be working on the same thing. This can create duplication of effort and role confusion.

Example: Requesting a Financial Review

- The finance committee argues that the early childhood program should raise rates for nonmembers.
- The early childhood program is studying the level of family engagement and trying to find ways to increase their connection to the school, to each other, and to the congregation.

Obviously both care, but who is responsible?

Just as staff supervision best practice suggests there is one person who is the senior partner providing direction to an employee, so task force initiatives need a responsible party.

Resolution: The early childhood program is the senior partner. When the early childhood program writes its report, they should request that the finance committee review their plan before they present it and provide feedback.

Example: Giving Advice
- The social action task force would like the religious school to explore doing more to support projects in Israel like Project Renewal or the Lone Soldier Initiative. The planning chair should ensure that this advice is considered.
- The religious school task force is looking at a range of informal education experiences that can increase student engagement. They are looking at a series of immersive retreats. They are exploring collaborative peer coaching projects that help students learn from each other and hold each other accountable.

Obviously both care, but who is responsible?

Resolution: The religious school task force has the ultimate responsibility to put this in their plan and to assign responsibility to staff and lay leaders. They should share a draft of their plan with the social action task force.

Going forward: It is the responsibility of the planning chairs to look for cases of role confusion. They need to look at areas that overlap and clarify how advice and recommended actions will be managed in the overall planning process.

Seeing the Financial Big Picture: The Assumptions List

The planning chairs should review all of the reports and list the financial assumptions for the budget that would be impacted by the task force reports.

Examples:
- The early childhood program looks to add ten new students.
- The facility committee needs to put up a security fence that has been requested by families for many years. Cost $10,000.
- Membership wants to reduce the minimum voluntary dues suggestion from $350 to $200 for young families.
- The FRD committee is going to create an integrated fundraising calendar. They believe they can raise an additional $50,000.
- The religious school committee is requesting an administrative assistant for the director of education. Estimate is $45,000.

After the Priority-Setting workshop the chairs will update this list and give it to the treasurer and the finance/budget committee, and copy the finance task force (if there is one).

Staging Task Force Reports

Task force reports need to be sent in advance of the Priority-Setting workshop to the task force leadership and the planning committee. It is true that in many cases the reports are not carefully read. Because there are always some careful readers, it will be helpful to let them use their gift for analysis prior to the meeting.

The Priority-Setting workshop is designed to use a variety of engagement techniques to ensure a high level of awareness of each of the strategic recommendations. Institutional leaders have seen many cases where the planning committee or the board has glossed over tough issues and reported out flawed plans because they were not willing to do the hard work of seriously reviewing the plans and considering their implications. How do we get key stakeholders to pay attention?

Mount Recommendation So All Can See

We are asking task force chairs to present only their top three to five priority strategic recommendations. Task forces should consider which will have the greatest possible impact.

The other recommendations and action items will be included in full in the appendix of the strategic plan.

Example of a Recommendation

Strategic Recommendation Title: *Develop a Membership Profile System for Members*

P—Purpose: Why? We are committed to understanding our members' interests, passions, and talents so we can better engage them.

A—Action(s)

- **What?** Develop a template for recording member profile information and a system to enter information.

C—Capacity

- **Cost:** $5,000 for software changes $$
- **Complexity:** CCC complex; requires a campaign to get information from members, manage it, and develop a cadre of people to match them to meaningful work.
- **Who?** Membership committee and executive director

T—Time

- **When?** Medium Term (MT): Seven to eighteen months

Sharing Vision and Recommendations

Each task force chair presents their strategic purpose and recommendations verbally to the group.

Welcome Questions and Comments

After the presentation, the task force chair welcomes clarifying questions and comments. A recorder should be assigned as a note taker for the meeting.

Integrate Recommendations: Look for Synergies

After all presentations have been made, the last conversation looks for synergies among task force recommendations. Are some actions dependent on others? Are there duplications in assignment of work? Which task force is best suited to take ownership of the recommendations? We have been encouraging the planning chairs to do this during the task force phase.

Voting on Recommendations

Planners pay attention when they are asked to vote! One way to reach greater clarity across the entire group is to allow each attendee to vote on the recommendations that they believe would have the greatest impact. Voting allows the entire room to see which recommendations have the most energy and interest of the group. There are pros and cons to including voting in your prioritizing meeting process (see below). Each person gets five voting stickers. We use Avery 0.5-inch round stickers (red or blue). They are instructed to vote for recommendations that will have the greatest impact. They can only vote once on any recommendation.

Cons

- Some task force recommendations do not receive many votes. Some leaders may then feel their work is being dismissed (even though all task force reports are heard and will be published in full in the final report).
- This kind of voting is not a scientific method. It is more of a "gut check" on what is most important.

Pros

- We have found that leaders focus their attention on others' work when they have to cast their votes. Helping leaders really honor and respect the work of their planning partners is one of the most important goals of the workshop.
- When voting is complete, the picture of clustered voting dots usually tells the story of what is emerging as priority issues for the synagogue for the next three to five years. This visual pattern can then be captured in narrative form in the executive summary of the strategic plan.
- Leaders have a tendency to make long lists of minor tactical improvements. Voting forces leaders to think about what initiatives would have the most impact.

Frustration at the Polls

At one priority-setting meeting we had a task force report that was very poorly prepared and unfocused. The task force chair had resisted attempts by planning leaders to clarify his report. It was a challenge for everyone to understand the recommendations being proposed under his area of focus, and some believed the recommendations belonged in other areas of synagogue life. When voting began, the task force chair was very agitated that no one was voting for his top four recommendations. It also made his task force team feel undervalued. As a consultant, I shared that our plan was to include all of their recommendations in the final report. This was a team effort to see what the group thought was most important. After the workshop, the president came up to me and said she thought it was a mistake to vote.

If a congregation does not want to vote, they simply look at the top one to two recommendations from each group and weave these into an overall narrative.

Priority-Setting Workshop

Workshop Agenda: 2.5 hours

Overview: 5 minutes
Text Study: 5 minutes
Review Reports: 90 minutes
Present: Three to five recommendations on PACT format

- One task force at a time: 5–7 minutes
- Feedback: 5–8 minutes

Group Reflection, Synergies, and Duplications: 15 minutes
Voting: 10 minutes
Break, We Tally Votes: 10 minutes
Reflection, Themes: 15 minutes
Close

Optional Exercise

Priority Assessment Matrix

- This exercise can be done at the workshop or later
- Take the top ten recommendations that received the most votes
- Place them on the matrix in terms of impact and complexity
- Impact means the ability to help us grow mission, members, or money
- Complexity describes how much cost in human or financial resources the recommendation requires

	Low Impact	High Impact
Low Complexity	Modest priority: Small but easy wins (Low impact: low complexity)	High priority: Drives Success (High impact: low complexity)
High Complexity	Very low priority: Poor investment (Low impact: high complexity)	Medium priority: Worthwhile challenge (Medium impact: higher complexity)

Assumptions

When all of the assumptions for new programs, services, and revenue and expense changes are explored, a number is given to the treasurer and the finance committee to put into a prospective budget. This allows leadership to explore the scenario envisioned by the planning committee.

Planners can consider all of the elements in the plan and consider the worst case and the best case for, say, fundraising and membership. This conversation engages all planners to gain a deeper understanding of the future.

Follow Up

- Have chairs make any changes, edits, or adds to the report.
- Summarize the votes.
- Consider creating an assessment matrix.
- Write up the emerging themes for your executive summary.

PART V

Lessons Learned

Chapter 17
Strategic Plan Report Writing and Plan Presentation

Joshua knows that the people need to have their values and goals repeated over and over. The desert wandering has many examples where God creates wonders for the people and shows that he will support them. Yet, over and over again, they lose faith and focus. When they turn their attention from the mission it leads to idolatry and sin. They even cling to an alternative vision of going back to Egypt. A slave's life is bad but you know when you will eat.

When he crosses the Jordan, Joshua takes the stones from the river and builds pillars and inscribes the law on them. He has the priests get up on Mount Gilead and Mount Ebal and call out the blessings and curses that will occur depending on how the people follow the plan. This is his vision statement.

He has the men born in the wilderness circumcised. He uses the power of sight, sound, and feeling to get the message across. There are moments in our people's narrative when little care is spent to orient and prepare leaders; however, Joshua makes a major effort to build commitment and explain next steps.

The planners have worked hard to shape a mission, vision, and strategy, but they will need to remind the people over and over about the possibilities of the future. Report writing is a key step in this communication plan, not a last one.

From Priority-Setting Workshop to Report Writing

At the completion of the Priority-Setting workshop, the steering committee, senior staff, task force chairs, and key leaders have created their recommendations for the next three to five years. Emerging themes lifted from the discussion will provide the narrative for the executive summary of the strategic plan. The communications and writing team is now ready to start assembling the strategic plan based on the information presented at the priority-setting meeting and from the various task force reports.

The strategic plan includes several elements of information. The areas that need description are included in detail here.

Strategic Plan Report Outline:

Welcome
- Letter from rabbi, president, and chairs
- Thanks to all: steering committee and task forces

Executive Summary
- Key steps in process
- Summary of overarching themes

Background to Plan
- Facts: data gathered from the fact book
- Situation Analysis: SWOT summary, highlight important findings
- Congregational Survey: executive summary of findings
- Community Conversations: executive summary of findings

Looking Forward
- Mission and vision

Priority Recommendations: Summary of Task Force Work
- Members
- Background
- Strategies
- Three to five priority recommendations for action
- Responsible party
- Time (ongoing, short term, medium term, long term)
- Appendix: full task force report

Large Congregation Example: Executive Summary and Plan Priorities

We held the Priority-Setting workshop on August 1 with the steering committee. They presented their top five recommendations. We then gave all participants five stickers to vote for the ideas that would have the most impact on finances, membership growth, and membership engagement. The following were the top five priorities.

1. Recommendation: "Put Our Members at the Center of All We Do"

We will create a system to identify the wants and needs, interests and passions of our members. We will then tag them in such a way that we can communicate to them about programs and engagement opportunities that will meet their needs.

With this member knowledge in hand, we will train staff and lay leaders to welcome them and to support them on a journey of deepening purposeful engagement.

What might it look like?

- We would connect youth that are in different neighborhoods, schools, and activities so they could be part of a larger synagogue youth community.
- We would help our families find their place in synagogue. We would invite them to tell their stories in our bulletins, on our website, and in hallways, so that people learn what the journey of deepening engagement looks like.

2. Recommendation: "Bring the Best of Our Past to the Service of Our Future"

Our synagogue has a long, rich history as one of the pillars of the Jewish community. It has many multigenerational families that have passed on a love of the synagogue to the next generation. In these times of change, how do longstanding stakeholders ensure that the synagogue will be able to fulfill this mission for future generations?

We will cultivate the commitment of longstanding stakeholders and encourage them to invest their time and money to sustain the synagogue by creating a legacy endowment for the synagogue.

We will utilize seasoned and experienced leaders to help ensure proper financial systems, oversight, and accountability and communicate to stakeholders progress on finance and governance.

What does this look like?

- Create and manage a legacy endowment to support our synagogue in the future.
- Create a team to review bylaws to ensure our synagogue's governance is aligned to fulfill its mission. Planning has provided a framework.

3. Recommendation: "Leverage Our Assets So We Can Better Fund Our Mission"

Our situation analysis pointed to our facility and our location as significant assets. As we try to invest in new programs, how can we leverage these assets and turn them into revenue? It requires a sense of opportunity and the will to invest in making these resources available for new purposes.

What does this look like?

- Invest to promote our outdoor space to hold children's parties. Possible annual income: $40,000.
- Invest to get certification for our kitchen so we can make our social hall a destination for celebrations. Could bring in over $100,000 a year.
- Invest in systems support to develop and maintain member information so we can leverage the assets of our members (talents, passions, etc.).

4. Recommendation: Plant Seeds for Future Leadership

Strategic planning is meant to look out five to ten years. How will we invest now for future developments? We will "greenhouse" new leadership by patiently developing it and giving it appropriate leadership and volunteer opportunities that best suit their talents and interests.

What does this look like?

- Bring youth together. Identify and cultivate young leadership.
- Bring emerging leaders together. Identify and cultivate emerging leaders to support affinity groups and committees.
- Reimagine the leadership program to teach leadership skills and help onboard new leaders and strengthen existing leaders.
- Develop key influencers who can help us gather information on their groups and promote opportunities.

5. Recommendation: Reduce Barriers to Spiritual Engagement

We will continue to work with leadership groups to explore the following:

- Liturgy
- Space
- Location

- Knowledge
- Length of Service

Full task force reports can be found in the appendix of the strategic plan. We are requesting that the strategic objectives and recommendations be approved by the board in total and communicated to the congregation at large. Members of the implementation team will report to the executive committee to ensure that the recommendations of the strategic plan will be carried forward.

Small Congregation Example: Plan Priorities

Our congregation is only twenty-seven years old and has seen steady growth in membership but with concerning trends in decreased school enrollments and youth programs. With statistics showing that now only about 30 percent of American Jews belong to any synagogue, we need to continually adapt to stay relevant to our current and future congregants.

Our core function as a congregation remains to be for prayer, study, community building, and social justice, and this guides our vision as we look to the future. Our strategy is to make our congregation the center of Jewish life for all of our congregants. We want to be the answer to the question of "why should I belong to a synagogue?" and for us to be able to easily articulate that vision to our current and future congregants.

Our strategic priorities for the future encompass three areas of focus:
- Congregant Engagement
- Financial Sustainability
- Human Capital

As our congregation ages, our first strategic priority for the future is for *young family engagement and recruitment* by creating:
- Creative financial models that make it less expensive to be part of our community
- Innovative and spectacular learning for our children
- A vibrant community for and to each other that teaches us how and why to infuse the beauty of Judaism into our daily lives

Our second priority is to ensure the vitality of our congregation through *strengthening our congregational leadership.* Thriving Jewish communities need great Jewish leaders to have the ability to face the challenges that we will be presented in the future. As such, we recommend investing in:

- Development, recruitment, and training for both lay and professional staff
- Growth of our current and future leaders

The board of directors, along with our professional staff and clergy, will work toward implementing our goals over the next three to five years. A major vehicle toward implementation of these goals will be through a Campaign for the Future that will enable us to raise the funds needed as well as generate the enthusiasm for the future that our founding families had when the synagogue was started in 1988. There are many recommendations that have resulted from our work, which are detailed in the following report.

Background Section

In the background section, writers should provide a synopsis of the data that was gathered on the historical trends, forces, and factors impacting the synagogue. Here are some of the *facts* that might be referenced (look to the fact book for the data):

- Membership trends
- Reflections on societal trends: external forces
- Enrollment trends for religious school and early childhood (where applicable)
- Dues income
- Other fundraising income
- Endowment growth
- Capital issues
- Deficit/surplus

Writers should also include highlights collected from other data-gathering processes, including the congregational survey, thriving congregation's assessment, committee interviews, and/or community conversations that support the strategic objectives and recommendations that are being presented for approval. Much of this was covered in the Emerging Themes workshop.

Additionally, writers of the plan will capture some initial reflections and include a short summary in their background:

(Example Short Summary from Data) What should we do next?

Respondents want vision and inspiration, with 96 percent believing it is most important that we give youth a strong Jewish identity and more than 90 percent wanting inspiring worship experiences and a sense of vision and purpose as Jews. Additionally, they believe it is very important to attract new members to the synagogue and greater participation of current members in programs and activities.

Respondents seem to be interested in more educational opportunities—from Hebrew language and Talmud classes and "Jewish Holidays for Dummies" to cooking and parenting classes. There is also an interest in programs for older singles.

Themes that emerge from comments focus on more personal outreach to congregants to better understand where they are as people and Jews. This yearning for more personal outreach includes improved engagement whether they are involved in the larger Jewish community or the synagogue.

Strengths and Weaknesses

Share some of the key findings of internal strengths and weaknesses in this format.

Strengths	Weaknesses
▪ Functioning daily minyan ▪ Fairly constant Shabbat service attendance ▪ Vibrant Friday night service ▪ Nursery school ▪ Debt-free building	▪ Tired leadership: overtaxed ▪ Membership revenue doesn't match infrastructure costs ▪ Detachment of ownership from synagogue community

Mission and Vision Statements

The mission and vision team over the past several months reviewed and discussed several iterations of an emerging mission and vision statement as part of the planning process. In some cases, a mission statement will not have changed from its original form, but it should still be included and referred to in this section of the strategic plan.

Here are examples of vision and mission statements:

Vision
We cultivate a Jewish community of purposeful belonging. We inspire and support spiritual journeys by deepening relationships with one another. We believe it is at the crossroads of our spiritual paths that life's purpose and God might be found.

Mission
We empower individuals to connect Jewishly to something greater than themselves.

Vision Statements

Here is an example of a vision statement in bullet form from a vision builder exercise with the steering committee, board, and task forces:

Chesed/Tzedakah
- We dream to be responsive across our generations to the needs of those within our congregational community.
- We dream to create relationships with the larger community and work toward the universal aspirations for tzedek and tikkun, justice and repair of the broken places in this world.
- We dream to build on Torah inspired values of love and charity, caring for and serving the interests of all of our members.

Community/Welcoming:
- We dream to build a community of relationships in which each congregational member feels a deep connection with one another.
- We dream to create a congregation that is a welcoming center of activity for all Jews, regardless of language or ethnicity.
- We dream to create a magnet community for Jews outside our geographic area through outreach and relationship building.

Priority Recommendations

In this session of the strategic plan, writers include the strategic purpose of recommendations and the supporting action items that will make it happen.

Planners want to honor and share the work of the task forces, at the same time acknowledging that the implementation is the purview of the board and the implementation team.

It's important to note though that the board is approving the overarching recommendations, but the specific action item(s) can evolve as discussions during implementation.

Strategic Plan Presentation Strategy

Mazal Tov on reaching this point in your planning process! A lot of time and work has gone into planning and the steering committee, staff, task force chairs, and members should celebrate the success of a job well done.

With that said, the plan now needs to be approved by the board and communicated to the congregation. As we have been instructing all along the way, the board should be made aware of the work taking place during the planning process. They should also have been brought into key moments such as taking assessments and surveys, informing the SWOT, and building a vision. Many accepted an invitation to sit on a task force. Additionally, strategic planning chairs and/or a liaison on the steering committee have been informing leaders at board meetings. Unfortunately, even with all of these steps, we know that many board members are not paying adequate attention to the information that is being generated and shared. It is for this reason that the presentation of the initial plan should first be shared with the executive committee for buy-in, support, and constructive feedback. It is *not* the role of the executive committee to fundamentally redo the work of the steering committee or the task forces, but they can and should ask questions on items that need clarity or can raise major red flags.

Presentation to the Executive Committee

Goals for presenting the strategic plan to executive committee include:
- Provide feedback and support
- Secure strong endorsements for the plan (ideally unanimous)
- Make some adjustments (if necessary) before the board meeting

Pros

- More transparency in the process. Bring in key stakeholders and influence makers.
- *Some* will be careful readers and provide helpful feedback.
- Allows strategic planning chairs to do a "dry run" of presenting the plan prior to sharing with the whole board.

Cons

- Executive committee may hold up the timeline in presenting to the board. Need to give them a deadline for feedback.
- Some members might overreach on role of reviewing plan. Need to provide guidelines.
- This should not become a substitute for real board discussion and approval.

Presentation to the Executive Committee and Board: Show Big Picture

Send the final report in advance to allow "detailed-oriented" readers to have access.

- Focus on the executive summary at meeting: "view from the balcony space"
- Use PowerPoint to convey big ideas and images
- Emphasize high-impact recommendations

Board and Executive Committee Agenda: 60–75 minutes

- Overview of Process: 5 minutes
- Background/SWOT Highlights: 5 minutes
- Mission and Vision Statement: 2 minutes
- Plan Priorities: 30–45 minutes
  - Task Force Recommendations (Top Three Only): 5 minutes each
  - Ask for Questions/Comments
- Motion/Discussion/Vote: 15 minutes
- Next Steps: 3 minutes

Community Involvement

Once the board approves the plan, let the congregation know of success!

Town Meetings

We encouraged you to offer some town meetings to share emerging ideas with the community.

Once the plan is finalized, you can offer another round of meetings for those who are interested.

You can present the plan and welcome members to ask questions about different parts of the plan. You can welcome them to get involved in implementation.

Communications

Share the plan via email/brochure/High Holiday speech, etc. The rabbi or the president can share the materials.

Chapter 18

Implementation

Making It Happen

Our biblical narrative does not move in a linear fashion. The Jewish people have periods where they follow God's law, and then they slip up and go backward. A good leader may emerge, but they are not necessarily followed by an effective successor. While the people have an overall direction, which is to enter the land and build a just society that puts God first, leaders often take their eyes off the prize. Now that the strategic plan has been approved, our leaders, like their ancestors, will find that there is a difference between what they plan and what they end up achieving. Life and leadership encounter obstacles in the road. How do leaders develop the capacity to overcome resistance? It takes tenacity.

We see some answers from the tradition in the life of Isaac. Isaac followed a very transformative leader. His father Abraham envisions the role of the Jewish people as a light unto the nations and sets a bold course of action. He makes big commitments. He sets lofty goals and acquires wealth and lands. Isaac has to implement the plan. Rather than going forward to make even more change, he has to struggle just to sustain the progress that his father has started. He faces enemies who oppose him. He has suffered trauma that drained his energy. He now has to build his own family and then rework the land. We learn that "Isaac dug anew the wells which had been dug in the days of his father Abraham and which the Philistines had stopped up after Abraham's death" (Genesis 26:18). His adversaries are blocking up his life-sustaining wells, and getting the water flowing is job one.

The implementation committee has to help bring the plan forward, but this might require revisiting some of the work that has already been done. Leaders need to "redig" some of these "wells." The plan should give the leadership a sense of direction. Staff and lay leaders on the committee are going to put this plan into operation. They will find things that are unexpected. They will meet people who are enthusiastic for the goals and others who are dragging their feet. They will have some great successes and some unwanted unintended consequences. We talked about the synagogue environment as often emotional and nonrational. All those emotional forces did not go away just because you wrote the plan. You are going to move forward but you may have to redig the wells that your plan opponents tried to fill in.

You Never Warned Us

One executive director complained that we did not help him implement the plan. Most outside consultants are tasked with helping planners work through the key planning steps so they can create a report. Few congregations are willing to pay for them to hold the board's hand in implementation. At USCJ our model did not allow for us to keep working with congregations beyond a few check-in calls after the plan is approved.

This chapter warns of the challenges that might arise during implementation. It also suggests how an implementation team could help. It is fair to ask a consultant for a model for implementation, but leaders have to remember that first and foremost implementation is the responsibility of the board and staff and not the implementation team. Implementation teams can focus the work of the board and staff, but they don't supervise anyone. Neither the implementation team nor the consultant have any power to hold leaders accountable. Planning should increase the capacity of the leadership to create goals and hold themselves accountable for action. When a congregation does not know what is going wrong, they will turn to who went wrong. Planning helps leaders move from blaming others to looking at how they can contribute to an accountable culture.

Two Warnings

Anticipate Challenges: Have a full debate about the level of complexity of your goals and the capacity for you to do them (see chapter 16).

Get Organized: Build an implementation process that will keep leadership focused on working with the plan even after it has been approved.

Getting Organized—Create an Implementation Team

In order to get the best out of your plan, we are going to need some champions to keep the board and staff focused as they try to implement the plan.

Goals of the Team

- Help monitor progress and hold board and staff leaders accountable
- Advise the heads of staff (rabbi and executive director), the president, and the officers
- Celebrate successes publicly
- Address problems privately

Characteristics

- Credibility: people trust them
- Ability to be proactive
- Ability to motivate volunteers
- Conflict management skills
- Team oriented

Composition

We suggest at least two members and up to five people.

1. One of the steering committee chairs or a prominent member of the steering committee (to provide plan knowledge)
2. A past president (has credibility and political power)
3. The first vice-president (someone who will have to manage in the future)
4. A current officer of the executive committee
5. The executive director, if applicable (optional)

Challenges for Implementation: Lack of Capacity

During the planning process we ask all task forces to write up their goals in a common template. They are asked to look at their capacity to complete a goal.

1. How complex is the goal?
2. Do they have people who can be accountable to complete the goal?
3. Do they have the money for the goal?
4. Do they have the resources they need?

What does lack of capacity look like? Leaders don't know who is responsible. Many congregations write recommendations and don't spell out the committee or person who will be responsible. When it comes time to implement, no one is really willing to champion the recommendation or do the work. Here are examples of problems that lie below the surface.

SVP CASE

Volunteer Tracking: Off Track

Their plan called for a new volunteer management system. Everyone in the leadership was very excited about tapping new talents. Leaders suggested that they follow up on the one-page volunteer profiles they collected in the process, but they found that they didn't have any volunteers to work on matching prospects to work that needed to be done. The office staff was not consulted when the highly motivated engagement task force mapped out these grand plans for volunteer engagement. Now leaders find that staff are not prepared to allocate the time to input the one hundred profiles that were gathered during the process. Staff complain they don't have time. Others suggest that they would be willing if they had an effective system to put information in. They say that the current software is not set up for this work.

Finance Recommendation: Not My Endowment Campaign

One congregation recommended a major capital campaign to create an endowment that would provide ongoing revenue for the budget. No one disputed the importance of this. The plan required that board members solicit for the synagogue's endowment campaign. As they began to implement the plan, few leaders attended the solicitor training, which was designed to use the plan to inspire donors to support their dream. One past president grumbled, "We don't need to do that." It turned out that few were willing to work on solicitation. The task force had well-intentioned people, but none were proven fundraisers. A few leaders who were testing the capacity found that that major donors didn't want the pressure of a big campaign.

The Ritual Recommendation: Clergy Not Singing from Same Page

The whole steering committee felt that there was a need to create more opportunities for members to connect to ritual. Only about 15 percent of the membership came at least twice a month to Saturday services. Waiting for them to come on Saturday morning was not working. The cantor and rabbi were on the task force that recommended new experiments. Now they complained about people leaving the main service for the new lay-led library minyan. The rabbi complained that the library minyan was "not honoring our traditions over there." The task force had insisted that the rabbi and the cantor work together on the task force so they would have "buy-in." They had heard about terrible problems in other congregations where lay leaders excluded clergy and did much of the work on their own. While the clergy went along in the meetings, underneath the surface, they had reservations and doubts. Planners did not realize that the clergy were not sharing all of their concerns.

SVP CASE

Leadership Recommendation: AWOL: Absent without Leave

Board leaders were on the SC. The board participated in several workshops. Now the plan called for the monthly board meetings to be changed. The report called for more commitment from members. When it was time to call a retreat to work on these changes, many of the members who most needed to be there didn't come. When the president suggested they create a by-laws committee to reshape the board, these AWOL (absent without leave) members acted as if they were shocked. "When did we agree to this?" they complained. The wheels of change had to slow down to manage this resistance.

What Helps? Align Officers, Staff, and Task Force Chairs

We want to anticipate these types of problems. Some of these conversations should be convened before the final report is done. If this wasn't done, it needs to be done at the start of implementation.

- Purpose: Meet with teams to review task force reports
- Responsibility: Clarify who is responsible to implement—between volunteers and staff
- Dual Tracking: Get officers to report to the president and staff to report to the executive director or rabbi.
- Time: Clarify timeframe (short term: zero to six months; intermediate term, seven to eighteen months; long term, eighteen months+)

SVP CASE

A Successful Meeting of Minds

One congregation decided to take an important step before they finalized the plan. The president and the SC chair called a meeting of all of the officers of the congregation and the chairs of the task forces to review the implications of their recommendations. In some cases, the timeline for the recommendation was pushed back. For the most part, the officers embraced the goals and partnered with their staff partners to figure out how they would get this done. This team-building prework created much more support in the executive committee for the plan as they began to implement. Instead of competing with the steering committee, the meeting helped get the officers on the same page.

Track Actions

A: Action What to do?	C: Capacity Who will do it?	T: Timeframe When?
Develop plan to strengthen human resources. Establish "volunteer corp" committee.	Executive director. Volunteerism committee.	Zero to six months.

Create a Color-Coded Initiative Tracking Chart

- Red: Stuck, HELP!
- Yellow: Proceeding, Work in Process
- Green: Done! We are on our way, yay!

In the book *Nudge: Improving Decisions About Health, Wealth and Happiness*, Thaler and Sunstein write about things we can do to help people make better decisions by putting them into situations that encourage a certain action. They use the example of an individual retirement account (IRA). Once we agree to start withholding money from each check, few people stop the process; until that time, their saving may have been erratic. With the help of the IRA process they now have a saving habit. Most congregations fail to write out their goals or hold themselves accountable to review their progress. The planners have achieved a great deal by writing out plan goals. Now we need to set in motion a review process, like an IRA, which is more automatic. We want to develop a leadership accountability habit. The color-coded tracking chart is just one approach to help us create that habit.

The Accountability Review

- Present a list of recommendations/goals to the executive committee.
- Recognize success so others see it can happen. Consider using a color-coding system (red, yellow, and green).
- Publicize goals that are stuck. No criticism is necessary in public. Just communicating status will motivate people. Most people feel the need to get off "red category."
- Behind the scenes, the implementation team works with staff and board to get to the root causes of delays and help get the group "unstuck."

Dual Track Accountability

The implementation plan is based on the idea of dual accountability. The implementation team uses shared vision and goals of the plan to focus the officers and the senior staff to drive the plan.

While this is helpful in implementing the plan, these principles are important for the ongoing accountability of both teams. If the executive director, rabbi, and president are all tracking the same goals, it is less likely that things will fall through the cracks.

Focus on the green. Ask, "What is working well?"

- Who can we recognize?
- What will the positive impact be?
- What can we learn from this success?

Getting Unstuck

Identify the Challenges

- Lay resistance?
- Staff resistance?
- Lack of resources?

Communicating with the Board and Community

- Report the status of major initiatives (not all) as appropriate in the monthly bulletin.
- Highlight recommendations that have been completed.
- Thank those who worked to complete the task.
- When a recommendation is moving into action, let people know how they can help.

Chapter 19

Lessons Learned

Stepping Forward Together describes a generic template for creating a vision and plan for the future of a congregation. Some of the case studies come from my years at the Alban Institute, but most come from the past eight years I have spent at United Synagogue, where my colleagues and I developed a program we call Sulam for Strategic Planners (SSP), based on the template I've described. This final chapter is about our experience at USCJ with SSP.

The USCJ Experience

In 2013, we launched our first cohort of Sulam for Strategic Planners at USCJ with ten congregations primarily on the East Coast of the United States. Since then, the Department of Synagogue Leadership at USCJ has facilitated a full strategic planning process with over sixty congregations in eighteen states across the United States and one Canadian province. We have worked with synagogues from 150 households to 1,500 households, in large cities and small towns. Over the course of the past six years, our team has

- engaged over 600 people on strategic planning committees,
- engaged over 2,000 people in a strategic planning task force, and
- engaged over 5,000 people with one of our congregational surveys.

USCJ's SSP program carefully and deliberately guides synagogue leaders step by step through the strategic planning process. We provide a skilled consultant who serves as an advisor, coach, and facilitator of key sessions, but it is up to synagogue leaders to do the work. We do our best to assess readiness, but in a twelve- to fifteen-month process, things happen: a president resigns, a rabbi retires, the planning chair gets sick or has a death in the family, or there is a crisis in the community.

We have found that even with our attempts to assess readiness, our detailed structure, our intentional workshop design, and our trained consultants, about 10 percent of congregations that embark on SSP do not finish.

What We've Learned about the Process

One of the first things we explain to a congregational planning team is that the process is at least as important as the final report. We explain that SSP is less about conducting a survey or writing a report and more about ensuring important conversations take place about the future of the congregation. We often find that we need to slow people down in order to ensure that they don't skip these conversations in their eagerness to write their recommendations.

Here are some of the questions we ask in order to evaluate the success of the program:

- Did they recruit a planning committee?
- Did they engage the community in a data-gathering process?
- Did they have conversations to discuss what they were learning from the data?
- Did they engage the planning committee and the board in a visioning process in which they discussed their hopes and dreams for the congregation?
- Did they recruit task forces to do a "deep dive" into specific focus areas?
- Did the task forces have meaningful conversations and make some recommendations based on their discussions?
- Did the planning committee have a meaningful conversation about the task force recommendations and how to prioritize them?
- Did the planning committee have a conversation with the board and the staff about the recommendations and their role in implementing them?
- Did any new leaders emerge from the process, and have they discussed how to utilize them?
- Did the leaders take time to share their emerging learning with the congregation via bulletin articles and town meetings?

We know from our work in the field and from the final reports of the congregations that the answer to most of these questions is yes. This means that the process has succeeded in achieving some important outcomes. What congregational leaders choose do with the recommendations is, of course, up to them. We have taken them on a journey to determine the right questions to ask, engage the community in important conversations, and create recommendations that take into account their capacity. Unfortunately, we cannot control whether or not they actually do the hard work of implementation.

We also need to recognize that many of the forces synagogues face are outside their control (for example, young Jews moving primarily to large metropolitan areas, the increasing rate of intermarriage, changing attitudes toward organized religion, etc.). While some declining congregations may be able to delay the inevitable by creating strategies to mitigate the impact of these factors, there will be some that end up making the decision to move, merge, or even close. Those may in fact be the potential outcomes of a successful planning process.

What We've Learned about Readiness

We have learned a lot about what constitutes *readiness* for planning. Early on, we were not very selective in recruiting for our cohort. As we worked with congregations, it became clear that some were simply not good candidates for our full-length planning process. Some were too small and simply did not have the capacity for a long-term planning process. Others had weak professional and/or lay leadership and were not able to gather the support they needed to take on this kind of intensive project. We now interview the prospective planning chairs and the rabbi in advance in order to get a better sense of their capacity to do the work before accepting them into the program. We discuss the importance of readiness in chapter 5.

The one critical readiness factor that has been affirmed for us again and again is the quality of the strategic planning chair and that person's ability to build a strong planning team. The chair must have the respect of the leadership, be able to see the big picture, have the ability to recruit and lead a diverse and talented planning committee, inspire them to do quality work, and hold them accountable. We need the whole leadership to support the chair (recruiting, participating, providing administrative support, etc.) so they can go the distance.

Two Cautionary Tales

1. The Chair Who Decides to Do It All Himself

We were working with a small congregation of about 230 households in the South. The planning chair was a highly experienced professional with solid leadership experience, and he did a fantastic job with gathering and synthesizing the data. The data summary was in fact one of the best we had ever seen. As the process moved into the task force phase, it became apparent that most of the planning team had checked out and were not very engaged, but the chair was committed to seeing it through to the end. When it came time to write the final report, the chair did almost all of it himself. The report was of high quality and had some great recommendations. But by the time the report was presented to the board, the chair had completely burned out. Over a year later, we got a call from the executive director saying that they were stuck and were having difficulty implementing their plan.

2. Too Many Distractions Derail the Process

We were working with an East Coast congregation of about 450 households. The president was very eager to engage in planning and was very excited to be working with us. She got the rabbi on board and put together a talented planning committee. We had a good startup meeting and they began to collect some data. Before long, it became apparent that there were some serious personnel changes being discussed that were taking the time and energy of the president, the board, the rabbi, and most of the planning committee members. There was no way they could focus on long-range planning when they were dealing with major staffing changes and the community's negative reactions to these changes. The planning process went on hiatus and has not yet restarted.

Synagogues' Most Pressing Concerns

Not surprisingly, we've learned that most of our congregations have similar concerns, regardless of their size or where they are located. First and foremost, they are concerned about member engagement, financial sustainability, and ensuring a leadership pipeline. Many are considering alternative dues models or trying to find new income streams beyond membership dues; some are experimenting with alternative Shabbat services; and others are focused on becoming more welcoming and inclusive.

Data from the Congregational Survey

When we began SSP, we developed a congregational survey to be used as part of the data-gathering phase. Some congregations have chosen to use our survey, some have developed their own, and others have chosen not to do a survey at all. Our survey attempts to measure satisfaction with various elements of congregational life, feelings of connectedness to the congregation, and attendance at various services and programs, as well as some general attitudes about Judaism and Israel.

Of the fifty-one congregations who participated in SSP between 2013 and 2018, thirty have used our survey. Some only do our community conversation focus groups. In total, over 5,300 people have taken our SSP congregational survey.

Respondents to the survey were about two-thirds women and one-third men. The vast majority were married, over the age of forty-five, and had not served as board members. They represented a good mix of newer members and longtime members.

While 84 percent say that they are satisfied with their congregation overall and 72 percent say that they are very likely to remain members over the next five years, *only 41 percent say that they are "very satisfied" and just 47 percent strongly agree that they would recommend the synagogue to a friend*. These numbers are important because these "strongly agrees" are the congregations' "raving fans" (from Ken Blanchard's book by that name).

As Blanchard teaches us, in today's world, being satisfied is not enough. Synagogues rely on their strongest supporters to joyfully participate and welcome others enthusiastically. Members and leaders who are just satisfied don't inspire involvement. It is also important to note that only 25 to 35 percent of the membership generally complete the survey, and respondents tend to skew toward the older demographic. We often have to make a special effort to hear the voices of new members or young families by inviting them to community conversations. Some just won't do a survey.

Overall, most survey respondents give their clergy very high marks. They feel that the rabbi knows them and is responsive in times of need. Numbers were significantly lower, however, when asked how well they feel the lay leadership knows them and knows their skills and talents.

When asked how connected they feel to the congregation, just 39 percent strongly agree that they feel connected, and only 34 percent strongly agree that they have good friends in the congregation.

In our experience with congregations, we generally find that about 10 percent of adult members attend services on a typical Shabbat. Looking at our survey data, 31 percent of our respondents say they attend Shabbat morning services at least twice per month and 42 percent report attending at least once per month. Not surprisingly, those who are willing to take time to complete the survey tend to be more active and engaged regulars. This sometimes inflates the results on participation and satisfaction with ritual and other programs.

What Matters Most

When asked about the most critical issues facing the congregation, the top three responses were:

- Making the synagogue a place where everybody feels welcome
- Giving youth a strong Jewish identity
- Giving adult members a sense of vision and purpose

What We've Learned from the Thriving Congregations Assessment Data

While the SSP congregational survey collects data regarding attitudes and satisfaction of the *membership* of the congregations, we have another tool that we use to gather data from the *leadership* of these congregations.

Understanding that not every congregation that is interested in doing strategic work has the readiness or capacity to engage in a full twelve- to fifteen-month planning process involving broad participation, we developed an assessment tool known as the Thriving Congregations Assessment (TCA) discussed in chapter 1, which we use to engage congregations in more limited strategic work. Since 2016, over 2,000 synagogue leaders have completed some version of the assessment, either online or on paper. We believe that *every* congregation should take the Thriving Congregations Assessment and review the results as a board.

The following data represents 1,004 respondents from forty congregations who took the TCA in 2018–2019.

Strengths

Five areas where we found congregations were *strongest*:

- 94 percent agree clergy provide care for all in times of joy and sorrow (69 percent strongly agree)
- 93 percent agree they feel warmly welcomed when they attend services (68 percent strongly agree)
- 85 percent agree their community is inclusive of people with different needs (51 percent strongly agree)
- 85 percent agree the leadership knows them and knows their talents and interests (50 percent strongly agree)
- 84 percent agree the clergy have built trust and have the congregation's support (44 percent strongly agree)

Challenges

Five areas where we found congregations were *weakest*:

- 26 percent agree there is a system to find out members' skills and interests in order to match them with volunteer opportunities (only 5 percent strongly agree)
- 32 percent agree board and committees have goals and are held accountable (only 10 percent strongly agree)
- 34 percent agree that there is a pipeline of new lay leaders ready to step up (only 7 percent strongly agree)
- 41 percent agree the board or nominating committee recruits and trains new leaders (only 10 percent strongly agree)
- 44 percent agree teens feel comfortable in the congregation and are visibly engaged (15 percent completely agree)

These findings support anecdotal evidence that most congregations are very good at being welcoming and inclusive with their existing members and not as good at creating effective, goal-oriented, accountable, and sustainable leadership that utilizes the talents and skills of current members and new members. These skills and practices are foundational to the ability of the leaders to develop *bold* strategies and implement them.

Stories of Impact: 1. A Small Congregation Takes a Big Step Forward

"Going through Sulam for Strategic Planners has been the most innovative and transformative process our kehilla has ever embarked on." (Planning chair of a small congregation in cohort 4)

In 2016, we received a strategic planning application from a small synagogue on the West Coast of about 180 households. They were not in a metropolitan area, nor in a community with a large Jewish population. The congregation was not in crisis, but they had been experiencing declining revenue, declining attendance, and low engagement, and there was some tension among the leadership about how to move forward.

The congregation applied and was accepted to our program and asked one of their new, young board members, who was a well-respected business owner, to chair their planning committee. They also made certain that the rabbi and executive committee were on board and committed to the process.

They completed their plan a year later, in the summer of 2017, and it was approved by the board. Since that time, there has been a status report at every board meeting, and almost all of their initiatives have been implemented. These were some of the outcomes:

- A reenvisioned membership committee was created, with new people, a new mission, and new goals. Six of the eight committee members are brand new leaders who emerged from the planning process.
- The new membership committee implemented a system to follow up with prospective members by scheduling coffee dates with them and offering to bring them to Shabbat services.
- A new communication committee was established whose first project was a complete redesign of the website and increasing the social media presence.
- A brand new dues model was designed and implemented with great success.

When we asked if they could point to any examples of impact, that is, growth that came out of the strategic planning process, here is some of what we heard:

- Twenty brand new leaders were identified during the planning process and have subsequently become engaged in committees and on the board.
- Shabbat service attendance went up by 10 percent.
- After several years of declining membership, there was a net gain of twenty member households, an increase of more than 10 percent.
- Dues income went up by over 30 percent.
- People are still talking about the community conversation that was held as part of the planning process, which attracted over 120 people and led to deeper engagement of many who attended.

According to the planning chair, as a result of the strategic planning work they did with us, the leadership has been able to turn the congregation around. Membership numbers are up, dues revenue is up, Shabbat attendance is up, volunteerism is up, and people are much more engaged. In her words, "SSP changed everything!" In some plans everything seems to come together.

Stories of Impact: 2. A Congregation Builds a Community Based on Covenantal Relationships

"We are creating a community built on covenantal relationships because we believe we are a stronger community when we connect with each other and our sacred tradition." (Rabbi of SSP cohort 5 congregation)

This midsized East Coast synagogue joined our program in the spring of 2017 and their final report was approved by their board in the fall of 2018.

The strategic planning committee at this congregation spent a year and a half working through the program, refining their vision, holding community conversations, conducting a survey, interviewing stakeholders, and engaging task forces. They chose to focus their work on the areas of leadership and governance, operations and finance, spirituality, prayer, learning, member engagement, communications, and, as their rabbi explained, the "sacred relationships with one another" that are the "connective tissue" that bind all of them together.

One benefit of the strategic planning process for this community was that the planning committee, made up of a diverse group of individuals who did not all know each other, bonded as a group. There was a cohesiveness that resulted from working so intensively on this project together over the course of more than a year. Though this wasn't necessarily a stated goal of the planners, it fit nicely with the congregation's goal of building sacred relationships. Creating an immersive experience for the planning committee so they become a team is a core strategy of SSP.

In response to the planning committee's strategic recommendations related to leadership and governance, the board implemented changes in their governance structure to ensure that every board member has a portfolio and is working with a committee. They have also brought new people onto the board, some of whom came from the planning committee. This had the added benefit of ensuring that the strategies contained in their plan had the buy-in needed to move the initiatives forward. In fact, the newly elected president was a member of the planning committee and chaired the implementation effort.

Congregational leaders also worked to ensure that their budget included the high-priority items that came out of the planning process, and the new president committed to including a strategic planning update on the agenda of every board meeting in order to ensure continual progress on their objectives. The creation of these new board practices is what we refer to as creating a leadership Haggadah. In fact, as of this writing, all major objectives identified in the strategic plan are in process and moving forward, albeit cautiously, in order to ensure proper buy-in and budgetary support.

Stories of Impact: 3. A Large Congregation Perseveres Despite Major Crises

"Much as we often hear parents say to their children as they become B'nai Mitzvah, this document is not an end, it is a beginning. It is our wish that the lessons we have learned and the insights we have gained over the past year will help to guide [us], and it is our hope that we will continue in our efforts to listen to our congregants and to other constituencies so that we always keep in mind what is important to our community." (From the final report of an SSP congregation)

This large suburban synagogue in the east has a large staff, a large school, a very diverse membership, and lots of moving parts. The rabbi has been there many years and is much beloved by his community.

The task force areas they chose to focus on were Jewish life, volunteer engagement, financial sustainability, early childhood to bar mitzvah, and teens.

Just around the time that the planning committee was finishing the report and preparing to present it to the board for approval, two major crises occurred that could not have been predicted. One was a natural disaster in the area. The other was a serious staff issue.

These two crises could have derailed the approval of the plan and its implementation, but due to the increased leadership capacity that resulted at least in part from the strategic planning process, they weathered the crises and moved forward.

Speaking to them about nine months after the report was approved, these were some of the outcomes they mentioned:

- More people expressed interest in joining the board than ever before.
- Some new leaders who were identified during the planning process have taken on larger leadership roles.
- Based on feedback received during the data-gathering process, they have made significant changes in the preschool, which have been well received.
- They have rotated some folks off the board to make room for new leaders.
- They are working with their member engagement director to rebuild the chavurah (affinity group) program that had existed previously but had been dormant for many years.
- They have been working with the budget committee to ensure that the major initiatives that came out of the planning process have the financial support they need to move forward.

Conclusion

The vast majority of congregations that begin SSP complete the process and produce a plan. A handful (about 10 percent) do not. As consultants, it is our job to provide the tools and resources, facilitate key sessions, and help to create a safe space for important conversations to take place, but ultimately it is the congregation and its leadership that need to recruit the participants, review the data, make their own meaning, and do the work. They write the report. It has to be their words. We can't want a solution more than they do. This is their work.

One of the most critical lessons we've learned in doing this work with over sixty synagogues is that while many congregations do not have the bandwidth to engage in a full strategic planning process even with our extensive support, every congregation, regardless of size or location, has the capacity to engage in meaningful conversations about the future and take some strategic steps forward.

To date, over 10 percent of our affiliated congregations have engaged in a full strategic planning process with us, and an additional 10 to 15 percent having done more limited strategic work with our tools and support. More importantly, we have taught synagogue leaders critical planning skills that they will be able to use throughout their own leadership tenure and pass on to the next generation of leaders. This book was designed to make these strategic thinking tools even more readily available. We welcome you to engage in strategic thinking. We encourage you to find other leaders so you can step forward together.

Chapter 20
Last Words

At USCJ, we always try to make the case that six hundred congregations know more than one ever could. In a Jewish world that is rapidly changing, we strongly believe that we are better and smarter together. Synagogue visioning and planning is based on the same idea that we need to mobilize all the talent we can in order to address the challenges of synagogues. We need to work to identify, recruit, train, and organize the talents of our staff, our members, and our community.

The creation and development of the steering committee, the involvement of the board and staff, and the empowerment of the task forces all build a guiding coalition that develops a shared understanding of the situation, a shared vision of the road ahead, shared goals, and shared accountability.

> Rabbi Hanina says that Torah is like a deep well whose waters were cold and sweet and delicious, but no one was able to drink from it. Then a certain person came along, and supplied the well with one cord tied to another, one rope tied to another, and drew water out of the well, and drank from it. Then everyone began to draw water and drink it. (Shir HaShirim Rabbah)

In SVP, the president, clergy, and planning chair are that "certain person." They step forward and look for all the different things that can make the rope longer. SVP is the process that helps leaders lengthen the cord. The water they seek is life sustaining. Water is also a metaphor for Torah learning. In order to be more successful, we need to work together to accelerate our learning.

The Spies: Reluctant Planning Leaders

In our biblical story, the spies function as a data-gathering team. When they return from their reconnaissance, they share their views and they create chaos.

They don't get all their facts right.

They lack a hopeful vision.

They have no process to debrief their data.

They have no plan to share the data with the community.

They have no goals for how to advance the mission.

They take no accountability for the future.

Jewish tradition does not move forward if the people stay in the Wilderness of Paran. The future is for those who take a risk to step forward and enter Canaan.

Moses falls short in preparing the spies for their task. When they return, they come back in chaos and spread their fear throughout the community, thus limiting the entire community's capacity for change. When planners are poorly prepared and led, they can set planning efforts back for years. In the case of the spies, their failure led to forty years of wandering. In that moment, Moses failed to lengthen the cord.

Joshua: Prepared to Step Forward

The Torah is full of texts of criticism and of consolation. One of Judaism's core beliefs is that people can learn from their mistakes. They can do *teshuvah*. They can revisit a challenge at which they failed and approach it with new wisdom and strength. After forty years of wandering, the negative leaders have departed, and a new generation of leaders has the potential to step forward.

Moses learns from his mistakes. He mentors Joshua. He blesses him. He presents him as a leader before the community. He honors him by letting him teach him Torah. Joshua internalizes this learning and steps forward with confidence. Just as Moses ritualizes his leadership transition, so Joshua will ritualize the people's entry into the land.

At the end of Deuteronomy, we hear a whole list of laws. In Ki Tetzei and in Ki Tavo, God explains what will happen if we don't take these laws seriously. He describes in great detail the choice before the people: a path of blessings and a path of curses. He reminds the people not to forget their covenant. Message: Don't Forget!

Joshua was mentored by Moses, so he has the mission of the covenant clearly in focus.

Joshua has the priests walk in front with the ark, and the people follow. When the priests put their feet into the Jordan River, the river parts. As we said at the beginning of the book, this moment recreates the splitting of the Red Sea. It shows that God blesses the people when they move forward with Torah in hand.

The people see that they are led by the Ark of the Covenant, they hear the words of the Torah, they feel the commitment to community. Joshua does all he can to ensure that they will not forget what Moses has taught them and that the people will not forget where they came from or where they are going.

Stepping Forward Together

In the first half of this book, we explained the challenges of exploring and managing change in congregations. In the second half, we provided a toolkit for leading this change process. Just as Moses prepared Joshua to lead, we have tried to prepare the steering committee to lead change. They create shared assumptions to develop a shared reality. They create a mission and vision for the road ahead. They train leaders to map out what needs to be done. SVP helps the congregation to understand their plan, using all of the learning tools we can muster. In doing this, we hope to help leaders part the waters of resistance and help the community to step forward into a blessed future.

Appendix: Resources

Resource 1

Attributes of Thriving Congregations

Please review the assessment and mark the box that represents where you believe your congregation is at the current time.

I. Foundational Practice—Communicate A <u>Shared Compelling Vision</u> of Purposeful Jewish Living	A Great Deal	Some	Little	Not Present	Don't Know
1. A Shared Vision—Leaders have gone through a **participative process** to create a shared Jewish mission/vision of *Purposeful Jewish Living* that connects them to the tradition, their fellow members and the world (ideally within the last 7 years).					
2. Visionary Clergy put Vision into Action—Clergy demonstrate how the mission and vision of the congregation can shape the community by "making the connection" through their preaching, teachings, and actions. They motivate lay leaders to put the vision to work.					
3. Stable Clergy and Staff Leadership Committed to Continuous Improvement—There is stable clergy and staff leadership with time to build trust, support, and leverage. They don't let up.					
4. Integrated Communications Plan—There is a team effort to tell a compelling story about how the congregation builds meaningful Jewish lives. It uses integrated communication, which connects website, bulletin, signage, and social media to make the case.					

II. Foundational Practice—Engage in Reflective and <u>Accountable</u> Leadership	A Great Deal	Some	Little	Not Present	Don't Know
5. Clear Expectations and Accountability—Lay leaders and staff have **clear job descriptions. They know who they report to** and what is expected of them.					
6. Reflective and Learning Leadership—Staff and lay leadership **take time to review** their environment, their organization, and their challenges. They evaluate programs and services to see what is working well. They **look for root causes of problems.**					
7. Sustainable Volunteer Lay Leadership—There is a **continuous pipeline** of lay leadership and volunteers. The Nominating Committee and/or a Leadership Development Team constantly identifies, recruits, trains, and engages new volunteers and leaders to go from generation to generation.					
III. Foundational Practice—Build Capacity to <u>Manage Change</u> and Conflict	A Great Deal	Some	Little	Not Present	Don't Know
8. Commitment to Innovation—Leaders seek to learn from others, and they are willing to experiment. They are **willing to risk failure** for worthwhile mission-based initiatives.					
9. Strategic Focus—There are strategic plans in place which help guide all leadership, clergy, and staff work. The leadership has the capacity to launch important task forces when they are needed.					

	A Great Deal	Some	Little	Not Present	Don't Know
10. Collaborative and Constructive Culture—Leaders look outside the synagogue for partnerships and collaborative experiences (either with other synagogues and/or organizations). They work inside synagogues to break down walls and create synergy by connecting departments. They can **manage conflict constructively.**					
IV. Foundational Practice— Ensure Sustainable and Sound Operations	**A Great Deal**	**Some**	**Little**	**Not Present**	**Don't Know**
11. Leadership Transparency Plan—Leaders ensure that key synagogue strategies, goals, and decisions are communicated to the entire congregation					
12. Financial Sustainability Plan—Leadership has created a viable sustainability plan that addresses membership, costs, and financial resource development. They have communicated the plan to the community. They have sound administrative procedures in place.					
13. Facilities Plan Provides an Appropriate Setting for Your Mission—Facility is appropriate in size and design for your community. Facility is attractive and welcoming. It supports your functions. It is in a viable location.					
V. Foundational Practice— Welcome Participation & Connection	**A Great Deal**	**Some**	**Little**	**Not Present**	**Don't Know**
14. Welcoming and Participatory—There is a process to welcome prospects, integrate them as new members, and help them engage and connect with the congregation over the life of their membership. Leaders have a sense of calling to widen the circle of active participants.					

	A Great Deal	Some	Little	Not Present	Don't Know
15. Community Engagement—There is an intentional process to **build relationships**. Leaders create **affinity groups** around demographics (young families, seniors, new members) and interests (book groups, field trips, cooking, etc.) so members can find a spiritual home.					
16. Help Engage and Connect with Families as they Transition through Life of the Community—Leaders have programs and services to engage families as they enter the congregation, early childhood programs, transition to religious school, move into youth programs post B'nai Mitzvah etc.					
17. Teen Engagement—There is a systematic approach to use informal and formal educational experiences to engage teens from post b'nai mitzvah through high school so that youth enter college with a strong identity. Leaders partner with camp and youth programs.					
VI. Foundational Practice— Motivate Deeper Engagement with Judaism through <u>Torah and Tefila</u>	A Great Deal	Some	Little	Not Present	Don't Know
18. Meaningful Engagement in Jewish Learning—There is a commitment to create lifelong learners. The congregation teaches key skills (Hebrew, liturgy, culture, history) and creates a passion to engage in meaningful learning. Learning leaders seek to connect with the whole family within the synagogue, at home, and in their community.					

	A Great Deal	Some	Little	Not Present	Don't Know
19. Meaningful Participation in Jewish Spiritual Life–Through a framework of Conservative Judaism clergy help members make the connection between "God's Torah based purpose" and their attempt to build a "life of purpose." They explore different approaches to prayer, within and outside the walls of the synagogue. They "weave a cloth of meaning" by connecting, prayer, learning, and social justice.					
VII. Foundational Practice— Advocate for Prophetic Justice—Covenantal Caring					
20. Israel Connection—Leaders connect the congregation to the land, traditions, sacred language, and people of Israel through programs, missions, and exchanges. Leaders help the congregation face the challenges and opportunities of partnership with the state of Israel.					
21. Caring and Inclusive Community—The synagogue community is inclusive. It has empathy for people with different needs. It reduces barriers for them. Lay and staff members provide care for all in times of joy and sorrow.					
22. Tikun Olam—The congregation has an external focus that connects them to the world. It has a deep commitment to tikkun olam and advocates for social justice (prophetic voice) outside of the congregation (larger general community, Israel, and around the world).					

Resource 2

Fact Book

Rationale for Fact Book

Strategic planning leaders must seek to develop shared assumptions that are based on facts, rather than opinion, about forces and trends that are impacting their congregation. A Fact Book organizes the data collection and recording process. As the process evolves, new facts will be added to the Fact Book. An initial review of the Fact Book is required pre-work before the Steering Committee does the SWOT (Strengths, Weaknesses, Opportunities, and Threats) exercise. You may not have all of this data. Make an effort to get the data you can.

INTERNAL

Age Demographics (individuals)

Data to Consider	10 years ago	5 years ago	Today
0–6			
7–13			
14–18			
19–24			
25–34			
35–45			
46–55			
56–66			
67–76			
76+			

Membership (per family units)

Data to Consider	10 years ago	5 years ago	Today
Membership history overall			
Family			
Individual			

Members with Children Living in the Home

Data to Consider	10 years ago	5 years ago	Today
Children under 17 in the home			
Children under 6 living in the home			

Describe Dues Approach:
Dues

Data to Consider	10 years ago	5 years ago	Today
Members by dues level			
Note: list your levels as you see best			

Data to Consider	10 years ago	5 years ago	Today
Number with dues abatement			
Percentage of members on dues abatement			

Data to Consider	10 years ago	5 years ago	Today
Number that pay premium dues above standard or sustainable dues level			
Dollars in premium dues levels			

Fair Share—As Percentage (If you have fair share.)
List number of members in different levels/groups (i.e. $1000-$1500 etc.)

Fair Share—Based on Sliding Scale Income
Provide scale and percentage of members at each level.

Members: Reasons for Joining
Why have they joined? What are the major reasons?

1.
2.
3.

Have these reasons changed in recent years?

Profile
What is the profile of the members who have joined over the last three years (ages, geography, religious background and practice, kids, etc.)?
Please describe.

Has the profile changed in recent years?

Members: Why do they leave?
Exit Interviews: Resignations—by type (moved, joined other congregation, cost, dissatisfied). What are major reasons?

1.
2.
3.

Other Data
Please provide any congregational surveys about members' wants and needs.

Summarize the key points of your latest survey.

Attendance at Worship Services

Data to Consider	10 years ago	5 years ago	Today
High Holidays			
Friday night average			
Friday night special programs			
Saturday morning – regulars			
Saturday morning with bar mitzvah			
Daily minyan			

Schools and Youth

Data to Consider	10 years ago	5 years ago	Today
Religious School Enrollment			
Pre School Enrollment			
Youth groups – USY			
Hebrew High School			
B'nai Mitzvah			

Education and Other Programs (attendance)

Data to Consider	5 years ago	Today
Torah study		
Adult education series		
Book groups		
Other		

Fundraising Contributions (dollars)

Data to Consider	5 years ago	Today
Contributions – dollar (Non HH)		
Capital contributions		
HH appeal		
Major fundraisers		

Fundraising Events

List top fundraising events and net contribution in dollars for the last three years.

EXTERNAL

Are there population studies from Federation? Review Federation information about where Jews are living by zip code.

Are there independent studies? Has the JCC or the day school done any studies?

Can we talk to other congregations about the size of their preschools, etc.? Are new people moving in, etc.?

Questions

What is happening in the overall economy?
Are jobs growing? Are housing prices rising?
Where are families moving?
What is the impact on schools?

Sources and Uses of Funds

Please provide a pie chart with the following breakdown of your budget:

Revenue

- Dues
- Fundraising events
- High holiday or annual campaign
- Program fees
- School Fees
- Pre-school fees
- Rent
- Endowment Contributions

Expenses

- Clergy
- Administrative staff
- Program staff
- Heat, light
- Building maintenance
- Insurance, legal, and accounting fees
- Interest
- Phone
- Other

Attach 1-page **Budget Summary** for current year

Resource 3

Member Profile

Name _____

Email _____

Cell Phone _____

Marital Status   Single Married Separated Divorced Widowed

Ages of Children (if applicable) _____

Current Job (if applicable) _____

Prior Professional Experience: _____

College Major (if applicable) _____

Graduate School Major (if applicable) _____

Growing up, what was your family's religious affiliation? (circle one)

Conservative Jewish   Orthodox Jewish   Reform Jewish

Other Jewish   Non-Jewish   Unaffiliated

Jewish Journey Stepping Stones

1. Please share at least one important thing about your background that has shaped your Jewish identity.

_____

_____

_____

2. Please share one interest you would like us to know about. (e.g., writing, art, business, literature, social action, text study, sports, etc.)

_____

_____

3. Please share one strength that you would like to bring to your work on the committee.

_____

_____

_____

Resource 4

Model Survey Questions

We suggest you consider some of these questions as the basis for your survey. Feel free to customize or add others.

Meaningful Connection and Engagement

Which of these factors are most important in your decision to remain a member of this congregation?

- The denominational affiliation of the congregation
- Location
- The clergy
- The religious school or preschool
- Friends and/or Family belong here
- Shabbat and Holiday services
- Other

Please indicate to what extent you agree with the following statements:

- I can articulate what makes this congregation unique.
- Our congregation is adept at managing change.
- The congregation is committed to innovation.
- When conflicts arise, they are managed constructively.
- We have a process to welcome new members.

Your Participation

In the past year, how often have you attended the following?

- A Shabbat or weekday service
- An adult education program
- A cultural event
- A holiday celebration
- A Brotherhood or Sisterhood event
- A board or committee meeting
- Other

Satisfaction

- How would you rate your overall satisfaction with the congregation?
- How likely is it that you would recommend this congregation to a friend?
- If you could wave a magic wand, what is one thing you would change?
- Is there anything else you would like to share?

Demographics

- How long have you been a member of the congregation?
- Please indicate your age (list various age brackets)
- Do you have any children living in your home? (list various age brackets)
- Do you have any children in our religious school?
- Do you have any children in our early childhood program?
- Do you have any children in our youth group program?

Resource 5

Model Congregational Letter

Dear Community:

At our recent annual meeting our chairs _____
announced the formation of a strategic planning committee that will spend the next year helping us look forward and plan for a thriving future for our congregation. Working together with the Rabbi, we have recruited a cadre of volunteer congregants who will coordinate the work of this strategic planning process.

Over the coming year, there will be a variety of opportunities for members of the congregation to participate in the development of our plan and provide substantial input. These will include interviews, focus groups, open forums, and a confidential survey. USCJ has done the work of developing this web-based survey for us, and they have tested it with a number of other congregations over recent years.

Within two weeks we will be sending an email containing a link to the survey. We will also have paper copies of the survey available upon request for those who would rather not fill one out online.

The survey will take about 10 minutes to complete and all responses will be confidential. The survey asks questions such as whether the programs, facilities, and services offered by _____
meet our members' needs. USCJ consultants will be helping us to compile the data and we will make a summary report of the results available to the whole congregation. This survey is a very important step in helping us to set the stage for our planning process, as it will be one of the ways that we identify key issues to address over the coming years. We hope that all members of the congregation will take the time to fill out the survey and make their voices heard.

We thank you in advance for your willingness to help out with this important process. Stay tuned for more updates on the process, as we head into the coming year.

President
Strategic Planning Chair

For Further Reading

Aron, Isa. 2002. *The Self-Renewing Congregation: Organizational Strategies for Revitalizing Congregational Life.* Woodstock, Vt.: Jewish Lights Publishing.

Aron, Isa, Steven M. Cohen, Lawrence Hoffman, and Ari Kelman. 2010. *Sacred Strategies: Transforming Synagogues from Functional to Visionary.* Lanham, MD: Rowman & Littlefield.

Blanchard, Ken, and Sheldon Bowles. 1993. *Raving Fans: A Revolutionary Approach to Customer Service.* New York: William Morrow.

Blumenthal, Jacob, and Rami Schwartzer. 2018. "Putting Mike Uram's 'Next Generation Judaism' to the Test." *eJewish Philanthropy*, March 12, 2018. https://ejewishphilanthropy.com/putting-mike-urams-next-generation-judaism-to-the-test.

Bolman, Lee G., and Terrence E. Deal. 2003. *Reframing Organizations: Artistry, Choice, and Leadership.* San Francisco: Jossey-Bass.

Buckingham, Marcus, and Curt Coffman. 1999. *First, Break All the Rules: What the World's Greatest Managers Do Differently.* New York: Simon & Schuster.

Butler, Lawrence. 2000. "Providing Meaningful Information for Governance." In *Building Effective Boards for Religious Organizations: A Handbook for Trustees, Presidents, and Church Leaders*, edited by Thomas P. Holland and David C. Hester, 204–10. San Francisco: Jossey-Bass.

Carver, John. 1997. *Boards that Make a Difference.* San Francisco: Jossey-Bass.

Close, Aimee. 2018. "Designing the Synagogue Member Experience." *eJewish Philanthropy.* https://ejewishphilanthropy.com/designing-the-synagogue-member-experience.

———. 2019. "Conversations That Matter: Five Years of Congregational Strategic Planning at USCJ." *eJewishPhilanthropy*. https://ejewishphilanthropy.com/conversations-that-matter-five-years-of-congregational-strategic-planning-at-uscj/.

———. 2020. "Design Thinking Techniques for Synagogues: Let's Talk Tachlis!" *eJewish Philanthropy*. https://ejewishphilanthropy.com/design-thinking-techniques-for-synagogues-lets-talk-tachlis/.

Collins, Jim. 2005. *Good to Great and the Social Sectors.* New York: HarperCollins.

Duhigg, Charles. 2014. *The Power of Habit.* New York: HarperCollins.

Eisen, Arnold M. 1997. *Taking Hold of Torah: Jewish Commitment and Community in America.* Bloomington: Indiana University Press.

Eisen, Arnold M., and Steven M. Cohen. 2000. *The Jew Within: Self, Family and Community in America.* Bloomington: Indiana University Press.

Gaede, Beth Ann, ed. 2001. *Size Transitions in Congregations.* Herndon, Va.: The Alban Institute.

Goleman, Daniel. 1995. *Emotional Intelligence: Why It Can Matter More than IQ.* New York: Bantam.

Heath, Chip, and Dan Heath. 2017. *The Power of Moments.* New York: Simon & Schuster.

Heifetz, Ronald. 1999. *Leadership Without Easy Answers.* Cambridge, Mass.: The Belknap Press of Harvard University Press.

Herring, Hayim. 2012. *Tomorrow's Synagogues Today.* Lanham, MD: Rowman & Littlefield.

Holland, Thomas P. 2000. "Developing a More Effective Board." In *Building Effective Boards for Religious Organizations: A Handbook for Trustees, Presidents, and Church Leaders*, edited by Thomas P. Holland and David C. Hester, 83–108. San Francisco: Jossey-Bass.

Holland, Thomas P., and David C. Hester, eds. 2000. *Building Effective Boards for Religious Organizations: A Handbook for Trustees, Presidents, and Church Leaders.* San Francisco: Jossey-Bass.

Jones, Steve. 2019. "U.S. Church Membership Down Sharply in Past Two Decades." *Gallup Organization.* https://news.gallup.com/poll/248837/church-membership-down-sharply-past-two-decades.aspx.

Knowles, Malcolm S. 1973. *The Adult Learner: A Neglected Species.* Houston: Gulf Publishing.

Kotter, John P. 1999. *John P. Kotter on What Leaders Really Do.* Cambridge, Mass.: Harvard Business School Press.

Kouzes, James, and Barry Posner. 2002. *The Leadership Challenge.* San Francisco: Jossey-Bass.

Leventhal, Robert. 2003. "Sulam for Current Leaders."

———. "The Accountability Plan." https://uscj.org/assets/resources/The -Accountability-Plan.pdf.

———. "The Change Management Plan." https://uscj.org/assets/ resources/The-Change-Management-Plan.pdf.

———. "The Delegation Plan." https://uscj.org/assets/resources/The -Delegation-Plan.pdf.

———. "The Leadership Plan." https://uscj.org/assets/resources/The -Leadership-Plan.pdf.

———. "The Lay–Staff Partnership Plan." https://uscj.org/assets/ resources/The-Volunteer-Staff-Partnership-Plan.pdf.

———. "The Volunteer Development Plan." https://uscj.org/assets/ resources/The-Volunteer-Development-Plan-Updated.pdf.

———. 2003. "Teamwork in the Synagogue." *United Synagogue Review* (Spring).

———. 2004. "Reimagining the Rabbi Lay Leadership Partnership." *Alban Weekly* (August).

———. 2006. "The Role of the Executive Committee." *Congregations* (Summer).

———. 2007. *Byachad: Synagogue Board Development.* Herndon, Va.: The Alban Institute.

———. 2017. "Strategic Planning Can Help Congregations and Its Leaders Thrive." *eJewish Philanthropy*, August 29. https://ejewishphilanthropy .com/strategic-planning-can-help-congregations-and-its-leaders-to-thrive/.

———. 2018. "Becoming a More Positive Leader." *eJewish Philanthropy.* https://ejewishphilanthropy.com/becoming-a-more-positive-leader/.

———. 2019. "Valley Beth Shalom Counseling Center Leadership Matters." USCJ.

———. 2020. "Emerging Leadership Lessons from the Crisis." *eJewish Philanthropy.* https://ejewishphilanthropy.com/emerging-leadership -lessons-from-the-crisis/.

———. 2020. "Seeing Like Barnes." https://byachadleadership.blogspot .com/2013/02/seeing-like-barnes.html.

Leventhal, Robert, with David Kiel. 2008. "Renewing Jewish Congregational Life Using Blended OD Methods: A Report from the Front Line of Community Engagement." *Practicing Social Change.* The

Practitioners Journal of NTL. http://www.ntl-psc.org/archive/renewing
-jewish-congregational-life-using-blended-od-methods/.

Light, Mark. 2001. *The Strategic Board: The Step-by-Step Guide to High-Impact Governance.* New York: Wiley.

Mann, Alice. 1999. *Can Our Church Live? Redeveloping Congregations in Decline.* Herndon, Va.: The Alban Institute.

Olsen, Charles M. 1995. *Transforming Church Boards into Communities of Spiritual Leaders.* Herndon, Va.: The Alban Institute.

Palmer, Parker J. 1998. *The Courage to Teach: Exploring the Inner Landscape of a Teacher's Life.* San Francisco: Jossey-Bass.

Parsons, George D., and Speed B. Leas. 1993. *Understanding Your Congregation as a System: The Manual.* Herndon, Va.: The Alban Institute.

Rabin, Joshua. 2016. "Will Your Synagogue Be a Club or a Cause?" *eJewish Philanthropy,* June 20. https://ejewishphilanthropy.com/will-your-synagogue-be-a-club-or-a-cause/.

Reicheld, Fred. 2011. "The Ultimate Question." *Harvard Business Review.*

Rendle, Gil. 1998. *Leading Change in the Congregation: Spiritual and Organizational Tools for Leaders.* Herndon, Va.: The Alban Institute.

———. 1999. *Behavioral Covenants in Congregations: A Handbook for Honoring Differences.* Herndon, Va.: The Alban Institute.

Rendle, Gil, and Susan Beaumont. 2007. *When Moses Meets Aaron: Staffng and Supervision in Large Congregations.* Herndon, Va.: The Alban Institute.

Rendle, Gil, and Alice Mann. 2003. *Holy Conversations: Strategic Planning as a Spiritual Practice for Congregations.* Herndon, Va.: The Alban Institute.

Sacks, Jonathan. 2000. *A Letter in the Scroll: Understanding Our Jewish Identity and Exploring the Legacy of the World's Oldest Religion.* New York: The Free Press.

Sales, Amy L. 2004. *The Congregations of Westchester.* Report on a study sponsored by the Commission on Jewish Identity and Renewal of the United Jewish Appeal Federation of New York.

———. 2006. *Synergy: Mining the Research, Framing the Questions.* Waltham, Mass.: Cohen Center for Modern Jewish Studies, Brandeis University.

Schein, Edgar. 1988. *Process Consulting: Its Role in Organizational Development.* Second edition. Reading, Mass.: Prentice Hall.

Schwarz, Sid. 2013. *Jewish Megatrends.* Jewish Lights.

Sellon, Mary K., and Daniel P. Smith. 2005. *Practicing Right Relationship: Skills for Deepening Purpose, Finding Fulfillment, and Increasing Effectiveness in Your Congregation.* Herndon, Va.: The Alban Institute.

Senge, Peter. 1990. *The Fifth Discipline: The Art and Practice of the Learning Organization.* New York: Doubleday/Currency.

Shevitz, Susan. 1995. "An Organizational Perspective on Changing Congregational Education: What the Literature Reveals." In *A Congregation of Learners*, edited by Isa Aron, Sarah Lee, and Seymour Rossel. New York: UAHC Press.

Snow, Luther. 2004. *The Power of Asset Mapping.* Herndon, Va.: The Alban Institute.

Telushkin, Joseph. 2000. *The Book of Jewish Values: A Day-by-Day Guide to Ethical Living.* New York: Bell Tower.

Teutsch, David A. 2003. *A Guide to Jewish Practice.* Second edition. Wyncote, Pa.: Reconstructionist Rabbinic College Press.

Thaler, Richard H., and Cass R. Sunstein. 2009. *Nudge: Improving Decisions About Health, Wealth, and Happiness.* New York: Penguin Books.

United Jewish Communities. 2003. *National Jewish Population Study 2001.* New York: United Jewish Communities.

Urban Institute. 2004. *Volunteer Management Capacity in America's Charities and Congregations: A Briefing Report.* Washington, D.C.: Urban Institute.

Wertheimer, Jack. 2000. *Jews in the Center: Conservative Synagogues and Their Members.* New Brunswick, N.J.: Rutgers University Press.

Windmueller, Steven. 2006. "The Second American Jewish Revolution." *Sh'ma* (June 2006): http://www.shma.com/june_06/second_american.htm.

Yoffe, Eric. 2005. Sermon. Union of Reformed Judaism 68th General Assembly. Houston, Texas. November 19.

Zevit, Sean Israel. 2005. *Offerings of the Heart: Money and Values in Faith Communities.* Herndon, Va.: The Alban Institute.

Index

About the Author

Robert Leventhal served as a sales and marketing executive for a cleaning products company, O-Cedar Brands, for nineteen years. He also taught marketing at the University of Dayton. For more than fifteen years Bob was a Jewish communal lay leader in Dayton, Ohio. He was a day school president and a JCC membership chair and federation campaign leader. He even taught seventh graders in his temple's religious school.

In 2001 he chose to combine his MBA and his master's degree in Jewish education to create a unique synagogue consulting practice at the Alban Institute in Herndon, Virginia. Alban was a research, publishing, and consulting organization that primarily served mainline Protestant congregations. Bob worked with congregations from all denominations.

In January 2012 he became the leadership specialist in the Kehilla Strengthening Department of United Synagogue of Conservative Judaism. He is the principal author, with support from USCJ colleagues, of United Synagogue's Sulam Leadership Curriculum (http://www.uscj.org/Leading Kehilla/SulamLeadership/default.aspx).

He is also the author of *Byachad: Synagogue Board Development.*

Contact Robert Leventhal at leventhal@uscj.org.